GREAT SCOTS

in the cookery business

BRIAN HANNAN

NEIL WILSON PUBLISHING · GLASGOW · SCOTLAND

Scottish Enterprise

Chefs

Neil Wilson Publishing Ltd
303a The Pentagon Centre
36 Washington Street
GLASGOW
G3 8AZ
Tel: 0141-221-1117
Fax: 0141-221-5363
E-mail: nwp@cqm.co.uk
http://www.nwp.co.uk/

Published in association with Scottish Enterprise and
the Scottish Chefs Association (tel: 0141-424-3371).

A catalogue record for this book is available from the British Library.

ISBN 1-897784-71-6

Typeset in Adobe Garamond
Designed by Janene Reid

CONTENTS

FOREWORD

Entrepreneurship in Scotland is alive and well! At the same time as more and more Scots are making the decision to start up in business for themselves in commerce and industry, so too are more and more Scots building successful ventures in the cookery business.

This book is the fourth in a series supported by Scottish Enterprise. The objective is to promote and publicise the wealth of talent amongst Scottish-based entrepreneurs and to demonstrate the variety of wealth-creating businesses which are being built by them.

The first title in the *Great Scots* series featured the 'big names' of current Scottish business, such as Tom Farmer and David Murray; subsequent publications in the series have featured young Scots entrepreneurs, and great Scots family businesses.

This book looks at successful ventures being built in the cookery and catering business. It is, of course, not only about great chefs and great food, but also about how successful and profitable businesses have been built around serving good food at the right price to the right market. For those aspiring to run a cookery-related business, this book is essential reading. But it has much to say to those considering starting in business for themselves, or who just enjoy visiting well-run establishments serving good food.

Read about Ronnie Clydesdale at the Ubiquitous Chip in Glasgow, who is credited with starting the Scottish culinary revolution. Find out how the Loch Fyne Oyster bar came into being to remind Scots about the value of fresh seafood. Discover Britain's 'King Curry' in Charan Gill of the Ashoka chain of Indian restaurants. And find out the secrets of the likes of Peter Bracewell at Drymen Pottery and Helen Ruthven at the National Galleries of Scotland.

More and more Scots are finding that starting in business for themselves is the right way for them; this book describes just a few who have done it in the cookery business.

Bob Adams,
General Manager,
New Ventures,
Scottish Enterprise

INTRODUCTION

Catering is one of Scotland's biggest industries. The growth has been created — like any industry — by entrepreneurs. But few people would be able to name many, if any, Scottish catering entrepreneurs. And there is a very simple reason for this. Few of the people featured in this book consider themselves entrepreneurs.

And there is a simple reason for that. Catering involves cooking, and cooking involves passion. In a business like that, there are rewards beyond money. Many people, even other caterers, believe that chefs and restaurateurs are in the business for reasons other than money. They forget that anyone in business has to make money. And in catering, as in any other business, some people are better at making money than others, better at spotting opportunity, better a developing new ideas, better at being entrepreneurs.

Also, catering entrepreneurs have tended to be faceless and while they might feature in the media it will not be in the business pages. But you will know them by their operations, by their brand names, by the names under which they carry out entrepreneurial activity.

Many of the caterers featured here represent some of the biggest names in the Scottish catering trade — Pierre Victoire, Braeval, Ashoka, Ubiquitous Chip, Loch Fyne Oyster Bar, Nardinis. Others such as Willow Tea Rooms in Glasgow and The Clifton in Tyndrum are local centres of excellence.

The Scottish catering entrepreneurial scene is a wealth of diverse opportunity and includes restaurants, hotels, outside catering, contract catering, museum catering, tea shops, and others which are not featured here such as sports catering and event catering.

This book brings together a series of profiles of some of the most dynamic entrepreneurs in Scottish catering. Many of them also led the way in new catering ideas through innovation and development.

Among those featured are Scotland's most famous chef Nick Nairn of BBC's *Wild Harvest* fame. Having set up the award-winning Braeval with his wife Fiona, a marketing graduate, ex-merchant seaman Nick identified television as a growth industry many years ago and developed skills that have seen him take centre stage in culinary Scotland. One of his mentors was David Wilson who, with his wife Patricia, added a deluxe hotel to his Peat Inn restaurant in Fife. And there's Ronnie Clydesdale whose Ubiquitous Chip in Glasgow kick-started the Scottish culinary revolution.

By contrast Anne Mulhern was a factory worker until, driven by love for the work of architect Charles Rennie Mackintosh, she opened the Willow Tea Rooms in Glasgow designed by him nearly a century ago.

Peter Bracewell turned his mother's gift shop business into a thriving tearoom in Drymen. The Wilkie family turned a garage into the country's largest stand-alone mini service station at The Clifton in Tyndrum.

Pierre Levicky runs a 100-strong chain of low-cost restaurants in Scotland, England and Belgium. Suzanne Ritchie set up a thriving outside catering and fresh meals business. Former shipyard engineer Charan Gill operates Harlequin Leisure, the largest Indian restaurant group in Britain. Helen Ruthven's company operates the catering at the National Portrait Gallery in Edinburgh. Andrew Lane and John Noble are oyster farmers turned restaurateurs, running Loch Fyne Oyster Bars in Argyll, Nottingham and Peterborough.

A year after she left college, Andrea Barton set up Barton's in Kirkcaldy. The Nardini family operate a chain of restaurants in Largs. Douglas Craig operates an outside catering business for whisky distilleries. Former accountant Mike Conyers is the man behind the D'Arcy's and 78 St Vincent St concepts in Glasgow.

Every new venture — whether in catering or any other industry — needs an entrepreneurial spark. Nobody quite knows where that spark comes from. But successful catering entrepreneurs share similar characteristics — determination, vision, focus, the ability to learn from mistakes, belief in their own ability and a whole raft of business skills acquired on the job.

The people featured in this book have come from a wide variety of backgrounds. Some have been in the business since leaving school, working for other people until striking out on their own.

Others have come from secure well-paid jobs in other industries, coming into catering with both the disadvantage of being a novice and the advantage of questioning accepted practice. Many of Scotland's best chefs such as David Wilson and Ronnie Clydesdale are self-taught. But virtually everyone in this book is self-taught in business terms. Hardly anyone has a formal business background.

By and large, catering entrepreneurs do it on their own with relatively little professional advice compared to other industries. There are fewer consultants in catering than anywhere else. There is no enormous wealth of data or studies into the operational aspects of this business the way there are for most other high-profile Scottish industries. And since operators often see another caterer as competition, there has been little grouping of resources and little common market research. The Scottish Chefs Association, which provides certain market data, only came into existence three years ago.

Despite this, there appear to be unwritten rules for success, if the case studies featured here can be taken as typical. Anyone thinking of setting up in catering will face many of the problems encountered by these entrepreneurs.

The main areas for any catering start-up are size, location, operation, menu, marketing, management and growth.

SETTING UP

Size is the key. But given that size equals cost, everyone starts out small with operations of about 20-40 seats (known as covers) and the number of covers dictates revenue. Given this fact, the bulk of restaurants on the market are similarly small. Location (see below) plays a major part in the start-up as restaurants in cities are generally more expensive to buy, lease or rent, than those in small towns, villages or rural areas. Restaurateurs typically own their properties.

Once you acquire a property, you have to fit it out, again generally out of capital, although there are some leasing schemes especially for equipment and you can buy second-hand from dealers or at auction. Fitting out can be expensive, but it can also be done cheaply, and most people starting out go for the latter option. Of course, if you buy a going concern, you can simply decide to retain all the previous occupant's tables and chairs and equipment. You may actually, cash-wise, have no alternative.

If you have to start from scratch, there is an extensive list of requirements. Front-of-house, for the dining area, you need seating, tables, cutlery, crockery, glasses, cruets, and, depending on the type of operation, perhaps table linen, napkins, breadbaskets. Unfortunately, many of these items break, go missing or are stolen, so you have to budget for replacements.

In the kitchen you will need cooker, oven, microwave, preparation areas, kitchen utensils, pots and pans, knives. You will also need storage facilities such as a refrigerator and dry goods store. If you are serving wine, you will need somewhere to store it, and wine racks, coolers, and refrigeration. Your staff will need uniforms (chefs' clothing is called 'whites') and the uniforms (and any other linen) requires laundering. Your dishes and glasses and pots and pans need washed — either manually or in a dishwasher. With growing concern about food poisoning, hygiene laws are getting tougher so you will need cleaning equipment. You also have to think of decor, but people starting out usually keep it simple. It's also worth bearing in mind that people generally go to restaurants for the food, and if the food is good, as Pierre Levicky proved at Pierre Victoire, the tables can be rickety. And you will need staff.

Remember also that you will be paying for the property from the moment of purchase, but you may not be able to open for several weeks and the gap between purchase and revenue generation has to be financed.

So the question of size is critical to the overall cost of setting-up the operation. Size determines potential. Your business plan is dictated by the size of the operation.

Often banks and other lenders will encourage first-timers to take out a bigger loan to operate a bigger business. The bigger the operation, the more expensive the fittings, the more staff are required and the more danger there is of food going to waste. The bigger the operation, potentially the more empty tables. And each table, full or empty, carries the same overhead.

But, in fact, a smaller business is usually a more sensible approach. The biggest ongoing cost is labour. Many start-ups dictate the size of their operation by their perceived labour outlay.

A couple with the ability to share the cooking and front-of-house tasks often decide that, in the beginning, they will operate with just the two of them, bearing in mind that simply to take on another member of staff they will have to generate greater turnover. People doing most of the work in their own business can also decide not to pay themselves the going rate, thus reducing their costs.

Some new operators are concerned about their ability to actually do the job, especially if they have switched careers. Often, especially given that business is usually slow at the beginning for a new restaurant, they decide to limit themselves to running either a lunch or a dinner service, or to close for certain periods of the week. Once they have more confidence or business picks up, they can decide to open longer. This sort of approach has other benefits, for during the fraught opening period, the new operators are guaranteed good time-off, and they don't find their confidence crumbling by having to stare at empty tables on quiet days.

Many restaurants just do it their way. The Peat Inn doesn't open on Sundays or Mondays because, in their rural location, they could never recruit the extra staff required to cover those days. Hilary and David Brown at La Potinière continue to run the entire restaurant — including washing up, hoovering etc — between them nearly two decades after they opened. No-choice menus are proving popular (Nick Nairn does this) because they save on food waste and allow the chef to better control the balance of a meal.

The Willow Tea Rooms offer afternoon tea in the morning and breakfast in the afternoon. The Ashoka has only a skeleton staff at lunch because there is little demand, and this allows his staff to work a 42-hour six-day week just in the evenings.

The type of operation you want to become depends upon experience and ambition. The main selling point of the bulk of restaurants in Scotland is simply the operation itself, whether its forte is cooking or atmosphere. The biggest revolution in catering in Scotland over the last two decades has been the growth of an indigenous culinary style, focusing on cooking Scottish ingredients in the Scottish way. In the 1960s, the chef was not a marketing tool for a restaurant. Now a chef's particular cooking style is the main attraction of many restaurants. In the 1960s, there was little room for originality. Now originality is everything. So there is far greater opportunity for someone to put their individual stamp on a business. But equally, there are plenty of role models to use as a starting-off point.

LOCATION

'Location, location, location' is generally perceived to be most important maxim of the hotel business. Its relevance to the restaurant business is less clear cut. The location of a new restaurant is usually dictated by what the new owner can afford.

The reason Scotland has such a diversity of excellent culinary establishments outside the major cities — for example, Nick Nairn at Braeval, David Wilson at the Peat Inn, Hilary Brown at La Potinière in Gullane, Jim Graham in Ostler's Close in Cupar — is that such premises were affordable.

Certainly few newcomers could afford a high street city centre premises. But cities are attractive because of what 'location' really means. In this context, location doesn't mean an idyllic setting. Location means it is on a busy thoroughfare, with a lot of passing trade (i.e. pedestrians), or close to large numbers of people, or in the heart of a business area, or easily seen from the road (i.e. motorists). This kind of location is important because restaurateurs spend relatively little on advertising and marketing. The bulk of the customers to most restaurants (unless upmarket) come from a small local area.

For some, a high street location is worth the risk. Others are simply more comfortable in a city. It is where they grew up, or worked, and they feel they know the marketplace and do not want to risk opening in an unfamiliar area. And every city has less expensive areas.

Rural sites are often attractive because they are surrounded by scenery. People with a dream of opening a restaurant often fall in love with a specific rural site, not realising that it is not an attractive location in the business sense. Rural restaurants have smaller catchment areas, and are usually less busy, especially at lunch. But they are cheaper and, by and large, staff will have better quality of life. Most city chefs can't see out of windows, while in the country chefs have more chance of looking out onto some scenery. However, rural restaurants have other drawbacks. Winter can be tougher in the country, sudden snowfalls or rainstorms can decimate bookings and drink-drive crackdowns have a bigger impact on business since there are fewer means of alternative transport. On the other hand, rural restaurants will tap more into the tourist market and can boom in summer.

But the aim of all restaurants, whether in the city or the country, is to become a destination rather than a location, when what you have to offer — whether the cooking, the decor, the atmosphere or the staff — is so good that people just want to come.

MENU

You are what you cook. Every restaurant is defined by the food it produces. But good food is not in itself a passport to success. Very often, the better the food the worse the business.

Planning and control are the most important aspects of the menu. Both concentrate on eliminating waste. After labour, food is the largest cost element in running a catering business.

The menus of too many restaurants in Scotland are simply too long. Unless an operation is offering basic dishes which need little preparation or cooking, then a long menu is a restaurant's worst enemy.

The most common complaint of restaurateurs is that they are generating turnover but not sufficient profit and that they seem to be working too hard. Both problems can be traced back to long menus.

Menus should not be simply a long list of dishes that a restaurant can produce, or create after a fashion. Menus should include only the dishes that are the best examples of what the restaurant has to offer. The menu is a selling tool and so is a satisfied customer. If a chef cannot cook seafood, there is no point putting it on. The secret is to offer what you are good at, otherwise logic dictates that the menu is composed of a great many dishes that you are bad at making, and what possible kind of advertisement can that be.

What stops restaurants cutting menus back is usually perceived to be lack of confidence. But it is more basic than that. It is lack of business skills. A restaurant is the equivalent to a factory selling direct to the public, in this case the product being food. Sticking with the factory analogy, can you imagine manufacturers producing products they know are substandard, or manufacturers keeping on product lines they know do not sell. Yet restaurants both sell poorly-made dishes and meals that do not sell. Manufacturers know their market and too often caterers do not. Restaurants with 40 or so dishes on the menu usually cannot list all the dishes in order of sales. They will know what their few best-sellers are, but they won't know what the middle-range sellers are or which dishes have slumped in sales simply because they have not invested, either by time or equipment, in any system of sales analysis. Looking at their bank statements is as sophisticated as their analysis gets. But restaurants which analyse sales find it easy to get rid of products and find it as easy to monitor the performance of new dishes.

It is also important to keep up with new food trends. Information in an ad hoc manner is relatively easy to acquire simply by reading magazines. The Scottish Chefs Association produces a twice-yearly *Scottish Restaurant Menu Trends Survey* which offers a more serious analysis of change. The latest report, for example, found that salmon and mushrooms were the top sellers.

Waste is the enemy of all caterers — wasted food and wasted effort. Long menus result in foodstuffs being unsold and thrown away. But long menus also commit a chef to too much effort for little return. All those dishes that do not sell are wasting his time, forcing him to maintain a series of skills the public does not want, when he should be developing specific skills and honing specific dishes to perfection. The smaller the menu, the easier it is all round, for the chef to have the time to develop his cooking skills, and for wastage to be brought under control.

The best restaurants operate quality control. New ideas will be tested out on kitchen staff and recipes tweaked accordingly.

A controlled menu offers more flexibility on pricing because less dishes means less fluctuation in customer demand. Caterers can learn how to create a menu composed of expensive and inexpensive ingredients. The general rule of thumb on pricing dishes is that the price the customers pays is three times the cost of the raw ingredients. This is usually the basis for most gross profit (known as GP) calculations. Most small restaurants don't bother trying to reduce this percentage, believing that somehow they will be cheating the public. But very often the discipline of trying to reduce the GP percentage does result in savings.

Fixed price menus and no-choice menus are becoming popular, both with the public and with operators. Fixed-price menus generally offer a choice of starters, main courses and desserts at an overall inclusive price (say £19.50 for three courses). No-choice menus offer one starter, one main course and one dessert for an overall inclusive price. Customers like this approach because they know exactly how much they will spend. Operators like it because the public likes it and also because it reduces wastage and because people eating three-courses are more likely to drink more. The caterer also has various options within both menu structures. The menu can be two courses (popular at lunch). Coffee can be inclusive or exclusive (adding another £1.50 or so to the bill, if exclusive). Upmarket restaurants usually offer complimentary tasters (known as an *amuse guele*) starter snacks and petit fours to give value-for-money. The *amuse guele* serves another purpose. They give the kitchen time to properly prepare the meal while the customer actually thinks the meal has begun. Taking drinks orders fulfils a similar purpose, customers think something is happening rather than just waiting.

Caterers need to forge relationships with food suppliers. Although there will always be bickering over prices, suppliers are the simplest source of information and advice. They know how other caterers use their products, and they know how best to use their own produce. Scotland has a huge number of small local suppliers who went into their business for the same reason as most caterers — a love of food.

MARKETING

The catering industry in general is poor at marketing. Unlike most other industries, owners balk at the idea of setting aside a percentage of their turnover to promote their business. The reason for this is embedded in a general lack of business skills, a certain reticence by operators to step into the limelight (partly for fear that it will backfire) and cost.

Where marketing does take place, it is usually in the form of advertising. But advertising is the most expensive form of marketing simply because operators cannot fix costs. Magazines and newspapers set the advertising rates and caterers must pay accordingly. Media advertising is generally not cost effective for caterers.

In general marketing, caterers have an astonishing edge over other industries for at the moment the media loves food and cooking. Huge amounts of television airtime are given over to programmes as diverse as *Wild Harvest, Taste of the Sea, Walk on the Wild Side, Light Lunch, Masterchef, Ready Steady Cook* and *Can't Cook Won't Cook*. Millions of people watch these programmes and television has made stars out of Gary Rhodes, Rick Stein and Nick Nairn. Each television series has its own best-selling book and newspapers and magazines run tie-in articles featuring such chefs. The television companies have marketing budgets, as do the bookshops and the magazines, to spend on promoting food and cooking. Monthly and weekly magazines feature recipes, every daily newspaper has a growing food section and then there are colour supplements and travel magazines.

So the media is already switched on to the cooking business. And acres of publicity can thus be obtained for nothing, available to any restaurateur who takes the time to go about it the right way.

The secret of success, as Nick Nairn pointed out, was access. He made a point of being available, no matter how inconvenient it was to him, to any journalist who called. The fact is, if you're not available, the journalists won't phone back. They have deadlines and little regard for inconveniencing anybody else. And journalists may well want something a restaurant considers beneath them — recipes for Xmas turkey or Burns Suppers or Easter bunnies. But reject a request for a Xmas dinner recipe and you won't hear from the journalist again.

Restaurateurs who get publicity in this way tend to get it again and again, while less co-operative chefs tend to mutter darkly about favouritism without realising why they are left out of the media mix.

It's also a mistake to think that caterers can only be reactive, that they only get publicity when a journalist phones up. Newspapers and magazines will respond to recipes sent in or pieces of news as long as this is not done indiscriminately and you have done your homework. If you don't know who to send something to, simply phone the magazine and ask. It's possible to build an entire year-round marketing campaign around this kind of free publicity. This is the best kind of magazine publicity because it is uncritical.

The other kind of free publicity — restaurant reviews — can be very critical. Again every newspaper and magazine of note has a restaurant critic. There is a trend towards the restaurant critic as entertainer, less interested in the food than in the words the writer can conjure up, but the bulk of restaurant critics are there to eat and comment. Good reviews bring in business. But bad reviews do not empty restaurants. You cannot hope — and should not dare — to try to influence restaurant critics.

Eating out guides also provide free publicity. There are guides to cover everything — from children's facilities and tearooms to pubs and restaurants. Guides are only too pleased to hear from you. If they don't know you exist, they can't review you.

Another good source of free publicity is winning awards. Again, there are mountains of award schemes. Most caterers would be surprised to know how few people enter awards. Most schemes give commended certificates, or an equivalent, so even if you don't win, you could gain publicity.

But very few caterers take advantage of this free promotion because they do not understand marketing, neither its benefits nor its drawbacks. Marketing is simply the promotion of product in a variety of means including leaflets, brochures, public relations, menu promotions and so on. It begins with a definition of the product, mainly by means of its strengths, and then identifying how best to promote those features.

As a business discipline, all caterers should know what their product is. But what they think it is may differ from the customer's perception because a caterer has not identified all the salient tools of marketing.

Marketing can begin, quite simply, by answering the phone. David Wilson says he takes every phone call, no matter what he is doing, at his restaurant because he is the best person to promote his operation. Many restaurants do not make the telephone a priority. In the morning, it is as likely to be answered by a cleaner. But a clear telephone statement can be the start of a marketing campaign.

Another simple marketing tool at a restaurant's disposal in the menu card. While any kind of menu costs money, every caterer needs to produce a menu and so greater thought going into the design and presentation of a menu can pay dividends. Some operators foolishly resent customers who ask for a menu to take away with them. Do they ever stop to think what the customer is going to do with the menu? Most likely, the customer will either be giving it to a friend or using it to tell a friend what a lovely meal they had. A stack of give-away menus, simply printed and perhaps in a reduced size, is a cheap investment.

After that, the cheapest form of promotion is a leaflet or brochure. Bear in mind that a large print run will properly maximise the setting-up costs. Leaflets can be left lying around for people to take if they wish, or they can be given away to every customer, or dropped through letterboxes, or sent out by direct mail.

Colour photography and a logo are also useful investments, despite the expense. They provide a real brand image and the logo can be applied to other items. The Peat Inn's logo appears on ties and other merchandising while copies of the photographs can be sent to magazines.

GROWTH

Entrepreneurs recognise opportunity. The direction in which a business develops can be the result of chance or choice. The entrepreneurs featured in this book have all added to their business, in both the apparent and less obvious ways. Entrepreneurs as diverse as Ronnie Clydesdale, Anne Mulhern, Charan Gill, Pierre Levicky and Mike Conyers have expanded their original catering concept into further sites.

Business development can equally come from a new direction. David Wilson opened a hotel, while Nick Nairn made a conscious decision to become a celebrity chef.

And entrepreneurs also recognise small opportunities can add revenue in a low-cost way. The entrepreneurs featured have also added sidelines that trade on the existing concept, exploiting its brand name, selling a different product to the same customer, but without adding any extra labour cost to the bottom line. Some of this is pure merchandising, but other ventures have become businesses in their own right.

Ronnie Clydesdale runs an award-winning wine retail business, Nick Nairn sold home-made tablet and parfait to retailers, Suzanne Ritchie has own-label herbs, Anne Mulhern sells tea-caddies, David Wilson sells ties. Such growth has been organic, often the result of a request from a customer.

The true entrepreneur responds by treating every request as a business opportunity.

Brian Hannan

PART ONE

Chef Restaurateurs and Hoteliers

REAPING THE WILD HARVEST
• *Nick and Fiona Nairn at Braeval* •

A decade ago, Nick Nairn was an out-of-work former navigation officer in the Merchant Navy. In the spring of 1996 he became Scotland's first celebrity chef with his BBC cookery television series *Wild Harvest*. Now he stands on the brink of superstardom, the first-ever Scottish chef to become a genuine brand name. And none of it is down to luck. Nick Nairn does not believe in luck. He believes in determination, application, hard work, and more hard work.

He was born in Bridge of Allan in 1959, the son of actor-turned-entrepreneur Jimmy Nairn, and left school at 17 years old and joined the Merchant Navy and got rebellion out of his system on a thousand salty decks and a thousand sunsets. In its place, he learned discipline, leadership skills, self-respect, and the value of application. He passed the stiff examinations for navigation officer and gained confidence and the knowledge that there was nothing more satisfying than doing your absolute best at whatever it was you were doing.

But when he came home to Scotland in 1983, he didn't know what it was he wanted to spend the rest of his life doing his absolute best at. He had taken redundancy from the Merchant Navy and was enjoying his freedom. He lived in a flat in Glasgow and took his turn cooking for friends. One day he decided he liked cooking for friends so much that he thought it was worth spending a chunk of his life on. As much as he liked the creativity of cooking, it was the mental challenge which exerted the greater pull. This was a job he would never stop learning.

Then, as now, opening in Glasgow was too expensive a risk for an inexperienced chef with nothing to lose but his life savings. He will admit to one piece of luck. His girlfriend, Fiona, was a marketing graduate. Fiona was born in 1961 in Glasgow, the daughter of an engineer with the South of Scotland Electricity Board. She grew up in Lanarkshire before taking a degree in French and marketing at Strathclyde University. She knew how to carry out the market research and develop the business plan they knew was essential for developing the right business in the right place. Just as important, she knew how to read the results of the market research and she knew how to say no to the wrong location and she knew that passion and commitment were not enough, not with so much at stake.

Turning away from Glasgow, they looked for a rural location where at least they could enjoy a good quality of life regardless of the expected turmoil of starting a new venture. Nick's father owned a derelict former Forestry Commission building just outside Aberfoyle. It was a good site, just off the main road from Glasgow to Aberfoyle and close to the M9 and Stirling. There was room for ample car parking out front. Fiona carried out a substantial piece of market research around the local area and nearby places like Bearsden and Bridge of Allan, going from door-to-door establishing if the residents would appreciate a new restaurant and what kind of food would they eat. The results were encouraging as was the fact — in the days before drink-driving — that 40 per cent of Scotland's population lived within a 24-mile radius of Aberfoyle.

Fiona devised a very detailed business plan, projecting a three-year cash flow with best/worst scenarios as well as a one-year day-by-day turnover projection based on covers and average spend. They knew that success would be based on a 65 per cent gross profit margin with wages limited to 25 per cent of turnover.

Even so, the project was fraught. Raising finance proved a nightmare as the couple were caught in the Catch 22 of the bank not committing a loan until the Scottish Tourist Board (STB) grant was confirmed and vice-versa. They spent one-and-a-half fruitless years trying to get money out of the STB, long after most people would simply have given up. Eventually, the Scottish Development Agency (SDA) came to the rescue by announcing a scheme for developing rural employment. The SDA gave a soft loan, deferring payments for two years with zero interest.

Even so, the couple had to come up with one-third of the total start-up cost. Then the hard work of rebuilding the derelict property began. Nick rebuilt everything virtually himself. The rebuilding went over budget by 8 per cent. The entire budget for outfitting the kitchen including all the cooking equipment was only £4,000 with only £2,000 left for tables and chairs with the consequence that virtually everything was second-hand. While the rebuilding was going on, they tried out recipes on each other to create their distinctive style.

Braeval Old Mill — as it was then called — opened for business on 12 June 1986 with Nick in the kitchen and Fiona out front. The menu was based on fresh food, cooked in a tasty manner — curried mushrooms with garlic mayonnaise, avocado and bacon salad with a strawberry vinaigrette — and little in the way of real culinary flair. The first night they invited the tradesmen with their wives and families. The objective was simply to survive, to manage the transition from domestic cook to commercial kitchen, to cook meals that were not burned, to cook food to order and on time. "The day before we opened", said Fiona Nairn, "all we wanted was to do a good job and win the respect of our peers. We hardly knew guides existed then and where else the business could go. We were also very hands-on, which is a distinct advantage for a small business. Examining accounts, I would search for a penny where a hired book-keeper might be inclined to give up, and in searching for that penny I might discover a couple of other things which could easily be overlooked. In a small business, it's the small things that are vital."

At that stage, Braeval was Fiona, not Nick Nairn. She was the smooth, charming front-of-house presence that kept the operation out of crisis. But she was also the sharp brain back-of-house, looking after the accounts and the bookings. And she was the smooth, charming voice at the end of a telephone generating media coverage on the back of a fairytale story of a young couple risking everything for their dream of a country restaurant. Most of all Fiona had done her homework, her market research had been accurate, and within ten days the restaurant was full every night. Lunches were quiet, however, and they were quickly dropped.

Six months later, they were still full, but it was clear that prices were much too low. They were generating turnover but no profit due to lack of confidence at the outset. They were faced with the prospect that what appeared to be success was actually failure in a cruel disguise. They put up the prices by 50 per cent. And held their breath. Customers kept coming. The business was afloat. But it was still too cheap and the gross profit was achieved by Nick doing all the cooking himself and by learning to buy well and by Fiona developing her skills as a manager and as the face of Braeval.

Between 1986 and 1988 the food was still simple, but better than the couple thought. The first awards started coming their way — in 1987 the restaurant won the Scottish Field/Newcomer of the Year Award and its first entry in the *Good Food Guide* — both for the cooking and for the restaurant. And they might have continued as a successful restaurant couple except that sometime towards the end of those first three years Nick discovered cooking — real cooking.

The couple realised something else about the life of a successful middle-of-the-road country restaurant. And that was that a 28-seater restaurant could not ever be a big financial success. No matter how successful they were, their success would only ever be moderate. And that it only took some outside force such as recession to rob them of even moderate success. Running a small restaurant in a rural area is beset with difficulties. Winter always presents a dilemma in terms of attracting customers. When the snow came, Aberfoyle was particularly difficult to reach from Glasgow and on many Fridays and Saturdays the full bookings turned into a half empty restaurant as cancellation after cancellation phoned through, or worse, did not phone at all. Those cancellations could not be easily replaced for Aberfoyle was too far away for people to go on spec. Summer was to some extent dependent on tourists and the tourist tide ebbed and flowed according to weather, the economy and, overseas, the state of the pound.

There was no money to do proper marketing. The best marketing was the free kind: word-of-mouth; reviews by restaurant critics; write-ups in eating-out guides and other articles in newspapers. But the danger, as Fiona knew only too well, was that this could be inconsistent and the critics could as easily be cruel as kind. What was more worrying was the understanding that the PR story was reaching its sell-by date. Most papers would only carry the young-couple-living-a-dream story once and the story itself only had legs until the next young couple came along touting a story along the same lines.

The worry of getting staff, a real anticipated area of concern, turned out to be fruitless as they managed to recruit locally. The other difficulty, ironically enough, was getting food, the raw produce without which there could be no meals on a plate. Good food suppliers were small companies like Braeval and didn't have the resources to deliver more than once a week. For larger companies, Braeval was too small a customer to offer a more frequent service. Not being on the coast, there were none of the local fishermen — the salvation of many a small restaurant — able to drop off seafood or fish at the door. Cultivating suppliers and to some extent educating them about the restaurant's needs was to become a growing difficulty.

They recognised that to become properly established, they would need a much higher profile. The obvious answer was to leave Braeval and start again in a city where weather, tourist traffic, and even supplies would be less of a problem. But they did not wish to leave Aberfoyle. A bigger venue in Glasgow would be a bigger risk and whether they lost or won in financial terms, they could only be losers in the quality-of-life stakes when they swapped the open countryside around Braeval for, most likely, a view of a busy road (for Fiona) and no view at all for Nick in, most likely, a basement kitchen.

Nick thought the answer was to stay put, but develop his cooking skills. Culinary skills had put other chefs in small rural locations — such as Hilary Brown at La Potinière in Gullane and David Wilson at the Peat Inn in Fife — on the map. He believed that suppliers would be keener to work harder for a really well-known chef and that having a good cooking name would attract chefs to work with him. "There are very few new start-up restaurants of our kind in Scotland", explained Nick. "A stand-alone restaurant has to be high-profile to survive. People will always come to a new restaurant, the secret is to get them to want to come back. But even then, you are very vulnerable. The only way to guarantee survival and success, we realised, was to become a destination restaurant, the kind of establishment that was on everybody's lips, but not because of any PR-driven hype, but because when they came the food was so good they wanted to tell their friends and, better, they wanted to come back."

Because of Fiona's background, they also understood the value of the media. One of the secrets of their success was that they were always accessible to the media, no matter how awkward it might be for them. When it came to trying to move into another league in terms of the cooking, they knew that the media could become even more valuable.

It was no coincidence that the changes at Braeval took place at a time when interest from all areas of the media in food and cooking was growing. Colour supplements sprouted regular food and cooking features and cooking was starting to move off the women's pages of daily newspapers. Radio started to have regular programmes. All of these produced a huge hunger for recipes.

There was a curious dichotomy in the minds of the feature editors responsible for putting together the content of the food-led sections of magazines and newspapers. Few feature editors actually knew a great deal about food and, at the time, there were almost no specialist food editors with any real commissioning authority. So their readers were fed a diet of articles and recipes that were almost in direct contradiction to each other. On the one hand, editors provided readers with recipes easily done in the home by any competent domestic cook. These recipes were provided by any number of freelance writers in the Fanny Cradock mould. On the other hand, the media featured a growing number of recipes by top-quality professional chefs which could be rarely cooked by the average housewife.

Editors were delighted to feature recipes by top chefs for two simple reasons. They produced very positive reader response. To understand the impact made by chef recipes, it's important to remember that in those days the average person believed that chefs kept their recipes totally secret. The other advantage for editors was more basic. Chefs gave their recipes for free. Top chefs were willing to spill their secrets and give up valuable time to pose with their dishes any way a photographer demanded in order to get free publicity. It was a wonderful arrangement. What was better, from the chef point of view, was that if you were featured in one paper or magazine, generally you were featured in others. It was self-generating publicity.

But editors understood the value of free publicity. They were not willing to give up valuable column inches and commission expensive photography to just any old chef. They wanted to feature only the best. So in order to capitalise on this growing marketing opportunity, Braeval had to become much better.

But something else was at work in the media. Television, the most powerful medium of all, had also woken up to opportunities in cooking. Almost as an antidote to the greed of the eighties, chefs were a perfect blend of craft skills and romance. The BBC series on the Roux Brothers changed forever the perception in the minds of chefs about the value of the media. Suddenly there was big money to be made. The Roux Brothers were paid for the television series and they were paid for the accompanying book. Television made the book a best-seller. Television and the book drove the public into the brothers' restaurants, Le Gavroche and the Waterside Inn. Television also made the brothers celebrities. For the first time professional chefs had access to the kinds of ancillary income that befitted celebrities. They could charge for their presence at an event, they could become consultants. They could make more money from being a celebrity chef than they could from just running a kitchen.

When Nick and Fiona changed strategy at Braeval in the early 1990s, it was with the aim of consolidating their business by raising Nick's profile and embracing the concept of 'Celebrity Chef'. "It appeared to be ludicrously ambitious", said Nick. "At that time, I wasn't remotely in the top league in Scotland and Scotland did not possess a celebrity chef in whose path I could follow. And it did seem that the most prevalent prerequisite for a celebrity chef was a foreign accent. But I always had total confidence in myself. I knew I could achieve what I set out to do and Fiona had a very sharp business brain. We are a great partnership. And I also knew that fashions changed, especially in television. There might come a time when home-grown accents were the rage. When that time came, I wanted to be there waiting."

For the first time, a real strategy emerged at Braeval, a concentration of effort that would produce effect, with everything worked out to the last detail. He even changed his name. He became known as 'Nick' in his business life as well as his personal life, realising that this was snappier and more appealing than Nicholas. Conveying just the right image for the nineties, 'Nick Nairn' was very user-friendly and easy to remember — being forgettable was not on the menu. He changed his hairstyle and got rid of his beard.

In the restaurant, the quality of the cooking went up by several notches. To improve his own skills and techniques, he worked in the kitchens of other top chefs. He brought home new ideas, fused them with his own. The change in cooking produced results. Accolades started flowing in. He was the youngest Scottish chef ever to be given a Michelin star (in 1991), the most important award for chefs since the judging system is run by the French. The star really put him on the culinary map. He had credibility in London and was welcomed by all the top chefs. The industry recognition was accompanied by media fanfare. In 1990-91, Braeval featured in virtually every magazine and newspaper in Britain.

It was an astonishing story. To the tale of the 'young couple opening a successful restaurant in the country against all odds' fairytale could now be added the rapid culinary rise of this ex-seaman. But there was a price. Encouraged by achieving one Michelin star, he set his sights on becoming the youngest Scottish chef to achieve two Michelin stars (the maximum is three, but the third star is generally for sumptuous surroundings and service rather than cooking) and almost went out of business in the process.

In chasing this dream, gross profit margins had gone out of the window. Staff levels had risen to the level of absurdity. This 32-seater restaurant was expected to support four chefs including two highly-paid chefs from London as well as its front-of-house staff. Worse, regular customers were frightened away by the complexity of the food. For a time, Nick was oblivious to the fact that the restaurant was losing money. In 1991, three overdrafts were extended until the day the bank called a halt. Braeval was about to go bust.

Overnight, Nick and Fiona changed tack. The costly staff had to go. Instead of chasing two stars, Nick settled for producing one-star cuisine (which still made him one of the top ten chefs in Scotland). But even with the staff cuts, they were faced with their original business dilemma, one shared with most small restaurants in Scotland. Could they find a way of making profit other than by chasing high turnover? Was there a way of maximising profit by reducing cost. In order to maintain even the one Michelin star standard, Nick needed quality support in the kitchen. He could not cook everything himself without collapsing from overwork.

The answer, it appeared, was to cook less. There was a successful precedent. A friend, Hilary Brown at La Potinière, was the only person in her kitchen and offered diners a no-choice menu. This was quite different from a set menu. Most restaurants offer set or table d'hôte menus (but often these have choices for each course) as well as a general or à la carte menu. The difficulty facing most restaurants is never knowing exactly what people will order with the result that more staff are required and there is always waste. Hilary Brown offered only one dish for each course — the diner has no choice. Apart from solving staff and waste problems, this approach had one distinct benefit for both chef and diner in that the chef can cook for the guest a meal balanced both in terms of food intake and flavour.

Nick and Fiona were on the verge of deciding they had no alternative but to try the Hilary Brown approach, providing a set menu without choice until pudding, when Nick had an accident in the middle of summer, their busiest period. This disastrous turn of events meant that it was impossible for Nick to continue cooking with the same menu format while up to his thigh in plaster cast. By unhappy accident, they were forced to adopt the new style and it is one they have stuck with ever since. More important, he went from being profligate to efficient. In order to produce this quality of food on all his own, he had to create a more efficient kitchen management system. And so he taught himself how to plan better, how to avoid crisis, and how to avoid waste.

Cooking less he could cook better. He had more time to learn and more time to experiment as he sought to move the emphasis away from presentation to flavour. But this mode of operation placed an enormous burden on the

• BRAEVAL •

Sample Menus

DINNER (Wed-Sat) £29.95
Game Terrine with Pear Chutney
Seared Sea Bream with Salad Nicoise
Roast Rump of Lamb with Pesto Olive Oil and a Tomato Jus
Caramel Mousse Brûlée with Caramel Parfait
Coffee & Tablet

SUNDAY LUNCH £21.50
Spiced Parsnip & Apple Soup
Lasagne of Chicken Livers with Lemon & Thyme
Fillet of Salmon with a
Mussel & Basil Butter Sauce with Savoy Cabbage
Ginger Tiramisu
Coffee & Tablet

WEEKDAY LUNCH (Thu-Sat) £18.50
Caesar Salad with Crispy Chicken Thighs
Roasted Cod with a Herb Crust, Piperade and Saffron Mash
Crème Brûlée with Rhubarb
Coffee & Tablet

chef. Since he was making all the choices, the customer had greater right to expect excellence. But Nick accepted the challenge. He and the customer were on the same wavelength. He wanted every dish to be the best every customer had eaten.

He increased his gross profit margin and improved the quality of service in the restaurant and the customers returned. With reduced costs, a better atmosphere and food the customers wanted to eat, the restaurant improved its operating profitability. He also sought to make every saving possible. He was obsessive about switching off lights and gas. He tried to extract every last portion from his ingredients. And he realised he could make small inroads into retail markets. He sold his own tablet and chicken liver pâté to retailers.

To maximise the slacker period in the middle of the week, he set up a cookery school once a week through the winter months. This proved extremely popular and provided Nick with the opportunity to work on his presentation and communication skills, so crucial for the next step the restaurant had to take.

Braeval had turned a corner. But they had not lost sight of their ultimate ambition. If anything, the restaurant had come out of this difficult period with a higher profile. They were aware that the restaurant attracted a lot of media people. These were people who liked cooking themselves. They liked talking to chefs. And Fiona and Nick were easy to talk to. Nature made them both very personable. And just as the media people started talking to the Nairns about the cooking business, so the Nairns started to talk to them about the television business. And gradually, they realised they had something in common.

Nick had total self-belief in himself. He was convinced he could become a television chef. He told people he was going to be a television chef. It might sound rather bumptious but he was encouraged when nobody disagreed. Television people don't encourage daydreamers. Everyone seemed to think, yes, he could be a television chef.

Occasionally, he was invited to be a guest on a cookery show and he learned about television exactly the same way as he learned about cooking. He knew nothing to begin with, but applied himself and saw it was a learning process. He saw that he could improve if he asked questions, whereas most chefs are too overwhelmed by the cameras to know that they have to project themselves.

The *Wild Harvest* programme was the result of endless discussions. It was a big risk for BBC Scotland because nobody in Scotland had made a cookery programme aimed at the network. And there was a fear that there were already too many cookery programmes — with Rick Stein, Delia Smith, Gary Rhodes etc. But the programme had a very distinct style and Nick had a distinct style that he worked hard to create. *Wild Harvest* started filming in autumn 1995. By that time Nick was also involved in *Ready, Steady, Cook*. The big danger then was that the restaurant could not cope with his protracted absences away filming. However, Nick had started to groom young chefs to help run the kitchen (one of whom was named Young Chef of the Year in the 1996 Scottish Chef Awards). Although no longer front-of-house on a full-time basis, Fiona kept the business on course behind the scenes, delegating the role of restaurant manager and working with the staff to ensure all ran smoothly. It's perhaps a measure of exactly how much Nick and Fiona have achieved that the television production work did not cause too much disruption in the restaurant.

When *Wild Harvest* was shown on television in Scotland in early spring 1996, it was a major success, with the highest-ever viewing figures for a launch programme on BBC Scotland. The series commanded a 20 per cent audience share when the target was 12 per cent. The book topped the best-seller charts. The series brought many new customers into the restaurant. The programme was then shown on national television in the summer and the book went into paperback. The national showing brought even more business for the restaurant.

A second series of *Wild Harvest* and a second book has appeared in 1997. Nick is also involved in three other television programmes. He also has a London-based agent who has offices in New York and Japan and his fee for celebrity appearances has risen substantially. He is also able to command considerable sums for consultancy work.

Nick and Fiona are both aware of exactly how much they have put into their business and are now looking at planning future developments. Success has not come overnight, but has been hard won. When they started out, they had no idea what the future would hold, and simply wanted to be good at what they did and to own a restaurant they could be proud of. "When we started out", said Fiona, "all we wanted was to succeed and survive. We gave ourselves the chance, took a risk and with a lot of hard work and commitment, we managed. The first year or two (if you last that long) are all about staying afloat. You have to be able to keep the ship on course and meet the challenges which you will undoubtedly encounter. How you face those challenges will ultimately determine your success.

"Thereafter, the spirit of the true entrepreneur materialises — you begin to relish the challenges, you seek them out and you have the confidence to go on to greater things. Braeval is our baby, the foundation of our business, but the future is bright and there are many opportunities waiting around the corner."

"People ask me if I ever thought in my wildest dreams", said Nick, "that I would be a successful television chef. But dreaming is not a formula for success. Perfectionism and hard work are. I'm an obsessive perfectionist. Everything I do I have to do really well. I work harder than anybody I know — twelve or fourteen hours a day, six or seven days a week. So people are surprised when I explain that it wasn't a dream but a business strategy, that I worked very hard at making it happen, that I created a brand called Nick Nairn."

AN UNLIKELY VENUE FOR A REVOLUTION

• Ronnie Clydesdale at The Ubiquitous Chip •

Revolutions have started in more auspicious places. But the Scottish culinary revolution began 25 years ago on 1 February 1971 in a former electrician's workshop in the West End of Glasgow.

The unlikely architect of change was a manager with a Scotch whisky company. In his mid-30s with no experience of catering, he was willing to gamble his redundancy cheque on the possibility that the locals might just appreciate good Scottish produce cooked simply and served without pretension. It was an enormous risk. Those were the days of flambé cooking, black-jacketed waiters bristling with authority, French menus with English subtitles, wine served in wicker baskets, invisible chefs, unsung ingredients, and hardly a whisper of Scottish cooking in the whole of the country.

It was against this intimidating background that Ronnie Clydesdale set up the Ubiquitous Chip, going resolutely against the flow. He had only an amateur's education in the culinary arts, cooking dinner parties in the unthreatening environs of his home. His research was rudimentary to say the least, long on instinct but short on anything resembling statistics.

On holidays abroad, he had seen how comfortable the locals were with their indigenous cooking and he saw that other countries, comparable to Scotland, had real food cultures based on a cooking heritage that no one automatically despised or treated with contempt. Italy and France had their own cuisine, nurtured with loving care over centuries and he wondered why Scotland, which was at least the equal of these countries in raw resources, lacked the kind of culinary tradition that had no problem fitting in with the commercial reality of eating-out.

Closer to home, he occasionally dined out as a perk of his job and was intrigued that his hosts, who ate out every day of the business week, were more interested in anything home-made on the menu than smoked salmon crevettes stuffed with prawns.

Lacking the blinkers of a professional chef, who would have taken refuge in caution, he saw cooking as an adventure and an exploration. The kitchen in the 48-seater premises in Ruthven Lane off Byres Road was cramped. Ronnie was the only chef and the cooker was a domestic four-ring model bought for a fiver from a house in Castlemilk. But he was very much on his own. There were no other chefs to contact for advice.

But he did know how much the restaurant had to take to survive. He relied on the most common kitchen calculation — that a menu was priced at three times the cost of the raw produce. And because he was the only cook, there was no waste whatsoever. And if he did something wrong, he wasn't aware of it because there was no one to correct his mistakes. He knew he would struggle with things that were second nature to trained chefs, but then trained chefs had no fresh ideas.

If he didn't know exactly what he was doing, he knew what he wanted to do and the menu said it all. The Ubiquitous Chip served up squid, pheasant, pike, salmon, salt ling and wild duck, all with stout Scottish origins, and vegetables like aubergines and courgettes that were so rarely seen in a Glasgow greengrocers that the market traders sold them under the label 'exotic'.

If the food was a reaction to the stultified menus of the time, the restaurant itself was a violent affront to the stuffy dining-room mentality of the period. The front-of-house style derived in equal measure from economic necessity, instinct, ignorance, and a deliberate attempt to re-think what the eating-out experience, from the customer's point of view, was all about.

He wanted to demystify food and eating out. He thought silver service was totally unnecessary, clogging up the actual service, and putting a barrier between the customer and the cooking. Bistros in France weren't full of waiters in dinner jackets lighting your cigarette and adjusting your napkins. He thought it was an idea whose time had come. He didn't think it would work anywhere else except the West End. He saw an opportunity which was quite hard to explain but in his mind it was simply that the restaurants one could visit in Scotland did not express the food culture which people wanted to see.

So front-of-house service was deliberately laid back so that customers did not have to endure the rigid formalities imposed by the waiting staff as the necessary requisite for a relaxing night out. Customers, on entering the Ubiquitous Chip, would be spared trial by maitre d'. The front-of-house was managed by a friend whose experience of catering was as scarce as that of her employer.

And if the waiting style was different, so were the people chosen to implement the change. For they were all women, an astounding decision in an era when front-of-house was dominated by men. Just as unusual was the fact that all the staff knew each other. Ronnie and his manageress had simply recruited their friends — a practice that persists to the present day and one which gave the operation a considerably more relaxed air.

The staff were also not trained waiters, with rigid modus operandi. Annabel, the manageress, was an air hostess, someone else wrote book reviews. The front-of-house staff were aware, educated, and at ease with themselves. In fact, the people who ran the front-of-house could just as easily have been eating in the restaurant. Staff did not have a service mentality. The staff were informal but informed. Nobody was called 'sir' or 'madam', there was no bowing and scraping, and no maitre d'.

The atmosphere was best described as 'hand-knitted'. Ronnie was reasonably competent with woodwork, knowing enough to make tables out of old frames. He bought in a job lot of mixed wooden chairs. Friends did the painting and the electrical jobs.

Guests were also allowed to bring their own wine, making dining out at the Ubiquitous Chip substantially cheaper. Wine glasses were provided and wine was opened and served free of charge. Coffee was not served in the usual demi-tasse but in decent-sized stoneware mugs made in an East End pottery. People shared tables and women on their own were made especially welcome — put at their ease by the knowledge that they would not be subjected by the all-female staff to the kind of unwanted attention that male waiters seemed to automatically bestow on single women dining alone.

The venture was completely undercapitalised, although he did have a sleeping partner. The banks, quite understandably, did not want to know. Most people thought he was crazy. With the famous maxim of 'location, location, location' the bedrock on which most restaurants were built, nobody could take seriously someone who wanted to open a restaurant in a cobbled dark lane. Ronnie had taken on a short-term lease. The first harsh reality of opening a restaurant was the knowledge that for the first two months of the lease there would be no income, that time being spent doing the place up. He had enough money to keep going for six months.

For the first three weeks on Monday to Thursday, once the preparations for service were complete, business was so poor that he would take a book and go to The Curlers pub in Byres Road and sit and read until the arrival of a customer necessitated his presence in the restaurant kitchen. For six weeks the restaurant struggled. Then, suddenly, it was busy. Suddenly it had become 'The Chip', a place to go, a place to be seen, somewhere worth talking about. By the end of the first three months, he had gone from sitting in the Curlers to recruiting staff to help in the kitchen.

Ronnie Clydesdale was born in Hillington, on the south side of Glasgow, in 1936. His Ayrshire-born father, who worked in the shipyards, had come to live with relatives in the city after being orphaned at the age of five. But it was his mother who exerted the greatest influence in terms of cultural roots. His mother's father was from Islay, but his death when she was thirteen seemed to make her keen to preserve her west highland heritage. Baking and high tea, to which hot food was incidental, was his mother's favoured entertainment along with Highland dancing and singing.

"When I came to cook decades later", explained Ronnie, "I seemed to know a lot about Scottish food without knowing why, as though I had a food culture inside me. My grandmother cooked salt ling, salt herrings, herrings in oatmeal, great soups, skirlies, and something called 'wee breeks' which I never quite managed to work out. I had never heard about clapshot (potato and turnip) which became one of our favourite vegetable accompaniments in the restaurant, but I knew about carrageen (seaweed), though I didn't know how I had acquired this knowledge. When I came to cook, I had a glimmer of the familiar.

"When I set up the restaurant, I was still learning. One great source of knowledge — and it still is for anyone setting up in the business — was my suppliers. For many of them, at that time, I was their sole catering client and they were delighted to dispense their knowledge". Ronnie added, "I tried to emphasise the origin of food. Perhaps this was marketing instinct, promoting something that was at that time unique, or perhaps I was just being evangelical on behalf of Scottish produce. Our menus revealed, in passing, the richness of Scotland's larder. Our menu was a statement not just for everything I believed in, but for a world of food I believed we could all share, a world that we could as Scots legitimately lay claim to, a food culture as indigenous as those I had seen abroad." He then added, "We always said on our menu — and still do — that it's Aberdeen Angus steak, Ayr-landed cod, Oban-landed squid, breast of Perthshire wood pigeon, breast of Solway Firth pheasant, saddle of Argyllshire venison, gigot of Renfrewshire mutton, and so on."

Having discovered his natural food roots, he set off on a culinary voyage of discovery through the Scottish food culture. And in so doing, he also discovered that using Scottish produce was a simple and very successful marketing ploy. He spent time trying out ideas which could incorporate Scottish ingredients into dishes that were not of Scottish origin. One of the best examples of this was barley risotto, created by the simple expedient of substituting rice with its common Scottish equivalent.

The restaurant has become famous for its haggis dishes — including an extremely popular vegetarian haggis. But the genesis of the dish was frustrating. He did not want to make it in a sheep's stomach. The eventual solution was to cook it using a double-boiler. The recipe is also quite unusual in that it uses no lights (intestines) and the ingredients include venison trimmings, heart and liver and a bit of mutton to sweeten it. The vegetarian version uses brown lentils instead of meat.

New recipes, new dishes, new ideas are the driving force behind any successful restaurant. He has a 'curious gift' for recipe development and his technique is unusual. He has a briefcase full of notes relating to new ideas and possible recipes that he accumulates over a period until he feels he has the germ of something. He always knows on paper whether or not the idea will work. He believes recipes are about making new connections. This is an instinctive gift, but borne out of years of experience and of trusting those instincts, and honing the skills until trapping those imaginative flights is second nature.

Sometimes the spark is easily traced. One time, he needed something to go with a wild mushroom starter. The solution came from Italy where he ate an unusual dessert of slices of aubergine salted and dried and dipped in egg like French toast and covered in chocolate with Strega folded in. Not necessarily the best dessert he had ever tasted, but it provided him with a possible connection. Out of this, he conjured up an aubergine custard to accompany the mushrooms. But other times the connection is less obvious. The restaurant's flan of peat-smoked haddie has curried lentils. But he has no idea what made him think of curried lentils. All he knows — all he needs to know — is that it worked.

The restaurant also has a certain loyalty to the idea of certain dishes. He believes that particular kinds of dishes — even if they don't sell in great quantities — should be represented on the menu of the Ubiquitous Chip. Among these dishes can be counted braised oxtail ragout or caramelised upside down vegetable tart with crème fraîche.

The early years of the Ubiquitous Chip were characterised by growth and the same spirit of adventure on which the whole enterprise was founded. This was nowhere more prevalent than in the area of kitchen staff. By the time business had grown to 112 covers on a Saturday night, Ronnie realised he needed more than himself, a lettuce washer and a dishwasher in the kitchen. Once again, he turned to people he already knew, for whom a couple of nights working in a restaurant fell within the boundaries of fun. In any case, amateurs did what they were told and they were unlikely to start questioning the head chef's methods. The restaurant did not hire its first trained chef until many, many years later. Now the biggest problems in the kitchen are maintaining quality control, ensuring that dishes are not altered.

But if the approach in the kitchen was revolutionary, so was the attitude front-of-house. Simply employing intelligent people as waiting staff was the smartest move Ronnie made. Intelligent people found solutions to front-of-house problems. The staff had a personal interest in making the restaurant work. They wanted it to succeed. They wanted, as potential customers, to go to a place like the Chip in Glasgow. Ronnie encouraged the staff to express their views. They introduced any number of ideas — from sea salt to wine vinegar — because that was the kind of thing the staff felt the Chip should have. The staff were empowered long before that was a fashionable — and mostly abused — management practice. If you put people in a position where they can only agree with you, you will not get the best out of them, and your business will not get the best out of its main resource — its staff. It never occurred to Ronnie to impose or enforce his views.

One great advantage was that none of the people he employed thought waiting was a menial job. Most of the women employed were very personable and confident, and they were happy to talk to customers about subjects of mutual interest. The great thing lacking in the Scottish restaurant business was the idea that you could serve people and still have dignity. Ronnie employed people who had natural dignity and made sure they didn't lose it.

"I would have been very foolish not to take on board the views of people like that", said Ronnie. "I wanted the waiting staff to know more about the

• THE UBIQUITOUS CHIP •

Selections from the Dinner Menu

TWO COURSES
WITH COFFEE & SWEETMEATS £26.60

THREE COURSES
WITH COFFEE & SWEETMEATS £31.60

Home-made Soup
Venison or Vegetarian Haggis and Neeps
Wild Mushrooms, Six Onion Pearl Barley Risotto and
Vegetable Crisps
Quail, Marinaded and Roasted, Watercress Custard
and Rich Game Reduction
Pan Fried Scallops (na Garvellach) on a roasted Potato Cake, Stewed Garlic
and a Chambery Coral Sauce

Free Range Perthshire Pork, Yellow Split Pea Pudding
and Bramble Compote
Wild Mushroom Custard with New Potatoes perfumed with Truffle Oil
Ayr-landed Cod on Clapshot with Roasted Peppers and Chilli Oil
Scotch Salmon Hot-Smoked on Darjeeling Tea with Buttery Savoy Cabbage,
Ayrshire Bacon and Mashed Potatoes

Caledonian Ice Cream with Fresh Fruit Compote
Scotch Madeira Trifle
Passion Fruit Burnt Cream
Orange and Olive Oil Sponge, Almond Tuille and
Beaume de Venise Syrup
Warm Pineapple in Balsamic Vinegar with Cracked Black Peppercorns
Scottish Cheeses

food than the customers and in that I was only developing their interests because I knew my staff had their own copy of Elizabeth David, that they gave dinner parties, that they scoured the colour supplements for food ideas.

"To get the service as casual as this and still make it work took a great deal of effort. We had to work out the best way to take orders, organise work stations and bills. I wouldn't say we came up with any unusual methods of running a restaurant, but what was unusual was that the methods were created by the staff in some kind of democratic process rather than imposed by someone like me from above."

From day one he employed people who could have been his customers and made sure that they understood the restaurant as customers as well as staff. They set up a system where staff could eat free in the restaurant from the main menu once a month and their partner could eat for a token price. This has evolved into what is easily the best teaching method — it has broken down the barriers between front-of-house and the kitchen. Food plated up in the kitchen always looks different once it reaches the restaurant and a chef who is eating as a customer then appreciates the input of the waiting staff.

One of the most satisfying parts of the system is that staff stay so long working for the Chip. It has become an extended family. Certainly, in the front-of-house area, almost all the staff are effectively recruited by people who already work there. There's no problem getting staff to work out front. Staff know they can go off and have a family and come back and work at The Chip later on. The one situation they have to confront head-on is how to properly delegate. He realised that he only thought he was delegating and had to sit down and really work out a system so that senior staff did not end up counting toilet rolls. There was a danger that people would bring problems to Ronnie that they should be able to solve themselves, simply because he was there.

"The one advantage of a chef running a restaurant is that a chef needs to be a good organiser to run a kitchen", said Ronnie. "You can be the best cook in the world but if you can't organise then you will fail. You need to be able to organise systems and people. You've got to be able to energise staff and make them pleased to do the work."

As the reputation of the Ubiquitous Chip grew, so did its business. After five years, the restaurant moved a hundred yards to the other side of Byres Road into larger premises in a former stables (for, curiously enough, Clydesdale horses) in Ashton Lane. The plan was for a self-contained restaurant to look out into a roofed-over courtyard giving a greater idea of space and relaxation. This plan was scuppered by the customers. Legend has it that one hot summer's day a customer moved his table out into the courtyard. Other customers followed. And suddenly 'The Chip' was a bigger, more attractive place to eat.

But the move brought other problems. The original Chip was very profitable because the food cost was totally controlled. And it was a long time before the new Chip became as profitable again because the volume of business was much bigger and with that came the problems of more food waste. Something goes wrong with the fabric of the building every day.

"It would be lovely if all you had to do was cook", said Ronnie. "But replenishing cups, saucers, ashtrays and cutlery, is an ongoing problem, mostly due to theft. The windows of the toilets were bricked up to stop people stealing chairs through the opening. And with it being a student area, toilet rolls are common targets for theft."

Further expansion was more organic. A pub with a 40-seater dining area and its own kitchen and menu was added in 1983. Customers now have a choice of four areas in which to eat — the original enclosed restaurant, the courtyard with its massive plants and pool stocked with fish, an upstairs gallery, and the pub.

The development of the pub came from Ronnie the entrepreneur rather than Ronnie the chef. Partly the idea stemmed from the attraction of the location. Glasgow University was one hundred yards away and many of its students lived within an easy square mile of the Chip. There was also a good chance of attracting the single well-off or young married West-ender. The pub would provide an extra revenue stream, generating income both from the bar and from food. While the pub menu was similar in concept to the restaurant, the ingredients used were cheaper. But the pub would also act as a feeder for the restaurant, introducing young people to the idea of the Chip, giving them a taste for that style of cooking. It was no surprise that come graduation day, the choice for a celebratory meal for the students was the Chip restaurant.

The restaurant has also evolved as a favourite of different cultural communities. As well as students, the media meet here, but so do artists and politicians. There's not many restaurants which boast an artwork by George Wylie or a wall mural on the stairs by Alasdair Gray, the artist and author of *Lanark*.

By now the management were looking to maximise the operation's potential and to expand in ways that were compatible with the restaurant's quality status and also to meet the needs of staff who wanted to further develop their skills.

There is no easier way to develop a business than listening to your customers. So when diners at the Chip kept asking where could they buy through a retailer the wines that they purchased with enthusiasm from the Chip's wine list, the opportunity seemed too good to miss. Like its food menu, the Chip had been innovative in its approach to wine. At a time when most restaurants just sold house red or house white, or marked up better bottles by ridiculous amounts, the Chip developed a more interesting list, marked by the owner's growing wine interest and educational development.

One other factor was that the wines on the Chip list were not generally available through off-licences. Scotland had very few shops devoted to wine at the time, most off-licences had little in the way of wine stock and even less enthusiasm for the product. By chance, a window cleaner's shop next door became available. This was snapped up, refurbished and opened as The Ubiquitous Chip Wine Shop. While initial custom came from the Chip's own customer base, the shop soon attracted its own following and has won many awards.

In 1994, Ronnie Clydesdale bought two restaurants — Back Alley in Ruthven Lane, the original site of The Chip, and The Spaghetti Factory in nearby Gibson Street, once the curry house Mecca of Glasgow. The Spaghetti Factory was transformed into Stravaigin', with a restaurant in the basement and a pub on the ground floor, featuring an eclectic menu cooked by Ronnie's son Colin.

Since its inception, over 800,000 customers — more than the entire population of Glasgow — have enjoyed excellent Scottish cuisine at the Ubiquitous Chip, in the process turning an unlikely dream into an institution. Last year, the Ubiquitous Chip received a Red M from the Michelin Guide, the first-ever restaurant in Glasgow to be so honoured.

But there has been a simpler reward for Ronnie Clydesdale in seeing his gamble succeed.

"There's not many jobs where you can get instant satisfaction from someone saying that the venison you had cooked for them was just gorgeous. You go home just bulging with pride."

ROOMS AT THE INN

• David and Patricia Wilson at The Peat Inn •

"It is very difficult to make money just running a restaurant unless you are able to do it on a large scale", said David Wilson, chef-proprietor of The Peat Inn. That was the situation facing David and Patricia Wilson, partners in The Peat Inn, in 1982. Against the odds, they had turned an old-fashioned ordinary pub into one of the most famous restaurants in Britain and put a tiny village in the middle of nowhere on the map.

They had a plan to radically alter the restaurant, but that, they felt, was not enough. A small country restaurant would always be vulnerable to recession and they could see that the changes in attitudes to drink-driving were beginning to have an effect. Their problem was the typical one facing a small successful restaurant. A business, any business, has to keep growing.

But all rural restaurants face particular restrictions. For a start, they are uniformly small, which made them affordable in the first place. They take longer to build up a reputation and it is very difficult for a chef-proprietor to move to a better location. The Scottish experience has been that wherever a chef opens his or her own restaurant, that is where they will remain. A chef-proprietor becomes identified with a particular location and becomes trapped by the trick of geography that embeds the place in the customer's mind.

The Wilsons wanted to take another route, following the common precedent set by chefs in France. They wanted to turn the restaurant into a restaurant-with-rooms and behind The Peat Inn create a small luxury eight-room hotel called The Residence. It would be the second biggest gamble of David Wilson's life. The biggest gamble had been sixteen years before when, at the age of 30, he had given up a secure job with one of the world's largest companies to try his hand at cooking.

David Wilson was born in Bishopbriggs, on the outskirts of Glasgow in 1939, the son of a glazier (who died when David was 17). His grandfather had set up the family glazing business John Wilson & Sons in 1895. David attended Bishopbriggs High School which he left at 16. He declined the opportunity to follow his brother into the glazing business and, instead, joined the firm of Fyfe & McGrouther, a wholesale industrial supplier, in Glasgow, at the same time taking a marketing degree at Glasgow College of Technology where he was awarded the Saward Baker Award for best student.

He married Patricia Docherty, whose father was an accountant with British Rail. She had a degree in printed textiles from the Glasgow School of Art. Later, they moved to Sheffield where he worked as area sales manager for James Neill, a manufacturer of tools and equipment. In 1966, he took on the position of marketing manager with a subsidiary of the conglomerate RTZ called Pillar Holdings which was in the pneumatic engineering business. There he was involved in developing the company's marketing strategy, new product development, and market research as well as working with advertisement agencies. He was responsible for introducing a corporate identity for the company and creating its company newsletter.

"But I was an impatient and impetuous person in those days", admitted David. "I couldn't stand waiting for decisions to be ratified by boards and committees. I wanted to be my own boss and it would have been impossible to start my own company in the area of business I was in. Patricia and I enjoyed eating out both in Scotland and down south. Cooking standards were by and large very low and I looked at cooking as potentially a business opportunity.

"I wasn't a cook. I really wasn't, not even the domestic kind. I didn't cook at home, Patricia did all that. Patricia was a good cook. When I decided I wanted to be a chef, I hadn't even experimented on friends at dinner parties. It was just something I wanted to do and thought I had the business credentials to make it work. Patricia encouraged me and pushed me to try."

Before taking the plunge, he decided, like any good businessman, that he needed to do some hands-on research on what professional cooking entailed. But that proved very difficult. At 30, he was far too old to be applying for a job as a commis chef, the most basic rung on the kitchen ladder. He was at least ten years older than his competitors for such positions. In those days, the kitchen hierarchy was strictly regimented, a system that dated back centuries. People entered a kitchen in their teens and worked their way up. It simply beggared belief that anyone of David's age could be serious in his job applications. Consequently, he was rejected for job after job.

Finally, he took another approach and applied, with Patricia, for a joint management position at the Pheasant Inn in Keystone near Huntingdon in Cambridgeshire. Not surprisingly, his application was rejected. But Patricia encouraged him to speak directly to the Pheasant Inn's owner Somerset Moore and explain what he really wanted. The couple were invited down for lunch and Somerset was so impressed by David's determination that he offered him a job.

The next eight weeks were the worst of his life. He was living away from home, didn't know anybody, and could not do the work for which he had sacrificed a good career. He was the oldest person in the kitchen. People a decade younger could do with their eyes shut simple jobs that he struggled to complete. And he had to cope with the mental shift from being boss to taking instruction in no uncertain terms. Eventually, it all began to make sense and his learning curve shot up so much that after a year he was made relief manager when the owner went on holiday.

But it was another year before he and Patricia could buy their own property. They resolved to be very well prepared on the marketplace before buying and bought all the trade papers to study restaurant prices. They wanted to open up in Scotland, preferably in or just outside Glasgow or Edinburgh but that proved beyond their price range. Selling their house in Sheffield generated £10,500 and with 60 per cent borrowings reckoned they could afford something in the £20-25,000 bracket. They scoured Scotland, looked at hotels, restaurants, pubs, even houses that could be converted, but without success.

In May 1972, they returned to Scotland anyway. David didn't have a job and signed on the dole. The unemployment people kept sending him for salesman's jobs and he kept apologising for wasting the time of people interviewing him and explaining his real ambition. One such interview was with Morris Furniture in Glasgow. Mr Morris was very enthusiastic and put him in touch with Freddie Levine, a Glasgow lawyer who loved food. Virtually the same day, the Peat Inn was advertised in *The Scotsman*.

David was struck by the advert. The restaurant was called The Peat Inn, the address was Peat Inn and the phone number was Peat Inn. If nothing else, it had marketing potential.

It turned out to be a rundown pub more or less in the middle of nowhere in Fife. But closer market research showed that it wasn't far from St Andrews, and the small town of Cupar was close by. It was on the market for offers over £18,500, well within their price range. His new lawyer Freddie Levine did the deal. Having bought it, they were almost prevented from opening. When David applied for a license, he discovered that far from being amenable, the local licensing board wanted to close the place down. Eventually, they agreed to give the Wilsons twelve months to make the necessary improvements. They got the license on 31st October 1972 and The Peat Inn opened for business the next day, on November 1st with a domestic cooker for the kitchen.

"I had a £5,000 overdraft from the bank and a £5,000 soft loan from the brewery", said David. "The bank didn't ask for a business plan. I didn't do a business plan right away. I phoned Freddie and he said I must have an accountant. He recommended French & Cowan in West George St. I went through to see a partner. He said the business looked healthy and that was it.

"It wasn't quite as slapdash as it sounds. The Peat Inn was a reasonably good buy, even just as a pub. It wasn't a disaster area. And I knew I had a sound business training that I wasn't going to ignore. I had a little knowledge of all the main business functions. I could do basic accountancy and had basic commercial skills and I had basic law. These were all old-fashioned skills that would serve me well in my new business", he added.

He then explained the key to his success. "I knew how to buy and sell. When it came to buying crockery or furniture or food, the same principles applied as buying machinery in my previous jobs — always shop around, make inquiries, do proper sourcing. Market research was second nature to me because I had been doing it for years. And my knowledge of accountancy was such that I could set up my own basic accounts without having to employ an accountant, an important saving when we were just starting out and money was tight. I also needed to be able to read figures so that I knew right away if something was wrong. There's no point finding out six months later when it's too late.

"Most important of all, I was able to deal with people. I had been a salesman, I knew how to communicate with customers and put them at their ease."

He added, "I didn't plan on just being a chef, I wanted to be a restaurateur. You can't make the jump from chef to restaurateur unless you have business skills. I didn't have the catering skills of young chefs who had attended catering college, but they didn't have my business skills. I had to go and work in a kitchen to find out how to be a chef and my advice to young chefs is to build up their business skills. A lot of business is common sense and you either have it or you don't, but there is also a lot you can learn if you're willing to apply yourself."

When The Peat Inn opened, there was just David in the kitchen and Patricia front-of-house, although Patricia also made the puddings in advance because she was better at this than David.

It's difficult to remember a time when pubs didn't serve food. Although in the early seventies English pubs were beginning to latch onto this new source of revenue, there was nothing doing in Scotland. Scottish customers were lucky to get a pie never mind a sandwich. So The Peat Inn made an immediate impact when it started offering about six dishes on the bar menu including home-made quiche, crab, home-made soups as well as puddings, and introducing wine into the bar. Almost everyone who came into the bar ate from the pub food menu.

They also ran a 50-seater restaurant in a long oblong room which had previously been used for functions and dinner dances. The restaurant menu had six starters, six main courses and five puddings. The tables were cramped together, but the food was cheap (90p for a main course, and 20p for a starter — an equivalent full meal today would be £5-6) and on a Saturday night some tables would be re-set and 60-70 customers served. Because the food was simple, service was quick. The operation ran seven days on the wet side and six days on the food.

The Peat Inn opened without any advertising or PR, but by the time summer came round word-of-mouth was all the marketing the site required. Summer (May-September, later May-October) became the peak business period. The business grew so quickly that David had to take on a commis chef to help in the kitchen within three months and shortly after more front-of-house staff were required. And it was equally clear that David had a real culinary talent to go with his business acumen. The Peat Inn was listed in the *Good Food Guide* within 12 months of opening.

By the end of the first year, turnover was £32,000, an improvement of £8,000 over the previous owners. Within two years, the Wilsons were in the black at the bank and able to invest £26,000 on improvements helped by a small grant from the tourist board, bringing the kitchen up to the best standards of hygiene, installing commercial cookers and central heating and moving live-in staff from caravans to three new rooms behind the restaurant.

David continued to improve his skills, coming up with ideas from books and magazines and from working in other restaurants.

But success brought other problems. The two parts of the business — the pub and the food — were at odds and attracted entirely different clientele. David knew from his business experience how dangerous it was to spread yourself too thin, how difficult it was to serve two markets, how easy it was to fall between two stools. Running a pub meant stress at closing time. After several years, the couple considered moving somewhere else and starting again, perhaps in one of the country house hotels that were beginning to become popular, or in a different location with a more upmarket operation. But they had built a reputation here and The Peat Inn at Peat Inn did have a ring to it.

They took the other option and stopped doing bar food in 1979. But this was just the baby step, in preparation for the giant step three years later. It was clear that improving the food and investing in David's culinary skills and rewarding their loyal customers with a smarter restaurant was the way forward. A country pub would struggle more than a country restaurant. A pub no longer fitted into the business strategy.

Now something more ambitious and long-term was being developed with a new business plan that would put the Peat Inn into a different marketplace altogether, turning it from the hybrid pub-restaurant into restaurant-with-rooms, a more appealing upmarket concept which had proven a successful route for French chefs.

"The idea stemmed from our holidays in France", explained David. "We often stayed in overnight accommodation run by the restaurant where we had eaten. The restaurants had recognised that they were the attraction for their customers, that people had come a long way to eat in their restaurant. But being in remote rural areas, often their customers had nowhere to stay, so the restaurants developed accommodation. Some of the rooms were fairly basic but since some of the restaurants were two- or three-star Michelin standard, their standard of accommodation reflected that.

"We thought we should do the same kind of thing. If we were to become a gourmet location, people needed somewhere they could stay." Income from rooms would help consolidate the business and make the restaurant itself more attractive since the nearest overnight accommodation was miles away.

It was intended that the restaurant would be more upmarket with rooms to match. The idea in 1982 was to spend £80,000 on a refurbishment of the restaurant and the kitchen (only about 10 per cent was spent on the kitchen) and £225,000 on adding rooms in a separate block. Patricia created an entire new look from furniture and carpets to lighting and table accessories. There were now starched linen white napkins, proper bone china and crystal glasses.

The restaurant upgrade was not aimed at multiplying the number of covers. In fact, seating was reduced to give customers more room at the tables and a lounge area was created where the customer could be welcomed in a manner more befitting the type of diner the restaurant's cooking had begun to attract.

From a business point of view, a comfortable lounge had other advantages — psychological, practical and financial. For a start, it would set the tone for the evening. The seating would be like a luxurious sitting-room, with deep cushions and a roaring wood fire giving off a distinctive aromatic smell and a wonderfully warm welcome on a cold winter's night. Here, customers would be offered the menu and have their order taken. They would sit in deep comfort until it was 'time' to go to their table. 'Time', in this context, would mean when the first course was ready. So when customers actually sat down to eat, there would be no delay in bringing the food. Equally, while customers were waiting, they would have a drink, perhaps a glass of champagne would be appropriate for the surroundings. When their meal was over, they would return to the luxurious lounge to drink their coffee, and perhaps a glass of port or brandy. The lounge would facilitate the overall service, add to the customer's enjoyment, and generate extra revenue without employing additional staff. On busy nights, it would also provide the opportunity to re-lay the tables, as both customers finishing a meal and new customers arriving would be happy to sit in the lounge.

The investment would be recouped by increasing the prices which the Wilsons believed customers would be happy to pay in return for better service, better atmosphere and better cooking.

The refurbishing was done in stages, by closing off particular sections of the restaurant, so that there was always cash flow. But it proved impossible to refurbish the restaurant and build the accommodation block at the same time. The hotel was a bigger risk than the restaurant upgrade. It was clear that David had substantial culinary skills which were being under-utilised in the pub-restaurant and would only really flourish in an out-and-out restaurant. It was also clear that his food could not be priced in a way that reflected its true value while the service standards were held at those of the pub-restaurant. But the pub-restaurant had attracted an impressive level of clientele who, it was clear, would pay more. So the restaurant development was underpinned by a clear business plan and strategy which could not be really faulted.

On the other hand, the Wilsons had no experience of running a hotel, let alone an up-market one. And, had the restaurant not existed, there would be no market for a hotel. Nobody in their right mind would build a small luxury hotel in the middle of nowhere. Worse, the Wilsons were going to target the hotel almost directly at their restaurant customers.

The hotel would only open on the same five days as the restaurant which was closed on Sundays and Mondays. Trade wisdom and common sense stipulated that a hotel that closed on a Sunday was not going to attract much weekend business. Worse still, the two-day closure would almost certainly rule out inclusion in the hotel guide books, an entry in which was long regarded as a foolproof way of establishing a small hotel. And since travel journalists used guide books as a major source of information concerning new operations, it was doubly dangerous. In addition, the hotel would only offer a continental, rather than a traditional cooked breakfast. And rather than maximising the available space, and therefore maximising income, by building 12-14 rooms, the Wilson wanted to make every room a suite, reducing the room capacity to eight, and to charge per-room rather than per-person. It was just too much and The Residence was put on hold.

But there were no doubts about the restaurant. Customers and food critics flocked to the new-look The Peat Inn. By 1985, the restaurant had gained a one star rating from the *Michelin Guide* (the bible for serious diners), the first restaurant in Scotland to ever receive this accolade (one other hotel had a Michelin star, but no stand-alone restaurant). And for a time afterwards, The Peat Inn was the only such restaurant, effectively making it Scotland's top restaurant. It also received two stars from the Egon Ronay Guide.

"This was our biggest change, and thankfully, it was generally well-received. But businesses have to change, and we never change, then or now, to please the public. We've never done anything for the public, we've done it because we wanted to do it, either for business reasons, or personal reasons, in order to stretch our culinary range. Customers generally don't like change, they don't see the need for it the way someone running the business does. Some businesses, especially in the restaurant trade, are frightened of change, but if you're frightened to change that means you're frightened of your customers and you'd end up losing control over your business. You have to learn to accept that customers won't like change right away. Customers get comfortable with what you have been doing and they don't understand why you had to change. We've not been frightened of losing customers by introducing changes.

"We were the first restaurant to stop serving side dishes of vegetables with a dish. We were following the French precedent, of course, but it seemed to us to make more sense to provide a different vegetable, chosen by the chef, to suit each particular dish. The customer actually gets to eat more vegetables and has a better balanced and more enjoyable meal. Why spend so much time thinking how you're going to cook a piece of salmon or duck or guinea fowl to get the best out of it if you're then going to absolve yourself of anything to do with the vegetables?

"We were one of the first restaurants to ban smoking, and restricted it to the lounge. That lost us a lot of business. You can't be all things to all people. We're not inflexible but we don't want to serve an eclectic menu with everything on it. You have to set out your culinary stall. If people like what you do, they'll stay. If they don't, you won't get them in by trying to guess what they'll like. We take a lot of risks, changing the menu daily the way we do. But good restaurants are not like mega businesses, with billions of pounds dependent on whether you can anticipate the next swing in customer demand.

"Restaurants are very personal. Customers either like what you do or they don't and often they can't put their finger on exactly what it is they like or dislike. Without trying to suggest we're remotely in the same league, customers react to restaurants the same way they react to movie stars or composers, they either like what the actor is doing or the music that has been composed or they don't, there's not a lot of analysis goes into it."

It took another five years to finally get The Residence opened. The delay was caused by a combination of planning difficulties and raising the necessary finance with the final straw being the discovery of old mine workings under the site of the proposed building. A further £20,000 was required to carry out the necessary civil engineering work and to pump some 400 tons of PFA (pulverised fuel ash) into the old mine shafts to consolidate the ground. The safety limit for this type of underground workings is 30 metres below the surface and the workings discovered here were 27 metres! This setback sent the Wilsons back on the hunt for financial help as the bank would not consider increasing its loan. A phone call to the local enterprise board brought a consultation, several meetings and some good advice on sourcing funds, helping the Wilsons raise £40,000 through both interest-free loans and low-interest loans involving a National Coal Board scheme (because of the mine workings) and Fife Enterprise.

The Residence finally opened at a cost of £300,000 with eight split-level suites. Interior design had been done by Patricia. The Wilsons had wanted suites, on the basis that this would make the rooms unique. The architect suggested that the suites could be split-level because of the way the land fell at the back of the site.

Rooms were split-level suites, they were sold on a per-room basis, there were only eight, there was no cooked breakfast, they were not open on Sunday and Monday, and they were not initially listed in any guides. But they turned out to be what the customer wanted. Even at today's prices (which have been held for three years) of £135 a suite (effectively £67.50 per person) for a luxuriously appointed suite with bedroom and separate living room, thick carpets and towels, elegant bathrooms and fittings, the rooms were a tremendous bargain.

David's business instincts were correct. As well as proving popular and relatively inexpensive for customers looking for somewhere to stay overnight, The Residence brought in other business. The opening coincided with more concern about drink-driving and generated more income for the restaurant. Staying overnight encouraged people to spend more on wine. It also brought more tourist business in the winter and mid-week. But the biggest bonus was from the business sector which could now be targeted for seminars and mini-conferences or for media promotions and for corporate entertaining.

"We did not ever want to run a full-service hotel", said David. "The idea behind a restaurant-with-rooms, which was our blueprint, was that customers who wanted to eat in a particular out-of-the-way restaurant could stay the night in accommodation that was better than basic bed-and-breakfast.

"But there were also very practical business reasons for our decisions. It's a very sound investment. We knew if it worked, it would work very well. But there was no point creating accommodation if all we could generate in revenue was £20 a night. People who wanted to pay £20 a night probably wouldn't want to eat at The Peat Inn, so there was no point in taking that approach. People who eat with us demand certain standards. We were better off having less customers paying considerably more. That way, we would have to spend less on staff and management time.

"The biggest risk was opening The Residence only five nights a week. But that was practical, too. We open the restaurant five days because to do otherwise would create enormous problems in terms of staff. Despite our reputation, we are off the beaten track. Getting and keeping staff was always going to be a problem. The nearest town is miles away and there is no public transport to speak of. We have limited staff accommodation. We work a five-day week so that we don't have to employ more staff and waste a lot of management time working out staff rotas and worrying about staff not turning up. Everyone works the same days, everyone has the same days off. It makes life very stable and it's very attractive for staff and, I have to say, for ourselves. Also, we don't offer a cooked breakfast because that would have meant opening up our kitchens and bringing a chef in to cook breakfast. But we do offer a wonderful continental-style breakfast with several kinds of fresh home-made bread, fruit compote, yoghurt, fresh fruit, cereals and orange juice and so on. Again, people like it.

"To run The Residence on any other principle would have been business madness. One of the benefits of having the rooms was that it allowed us to develop a better management structure. The rooms, although capital intensive, are not labour-intensive.

"By and large, everyone has accepted the way the operation runs. When we opened The Residence, we increased our level of marketing and that has had an extra benefit for the restaurant. We don't get the recognition we would like from guides, but we seem to get enough publicity nonetheless and it's easy enough to market to our existing restaurant customers who we identified as providing the bulk of our business anyway.

"We've always done our best to look after our staff. You need to respect your staff. Some need help, some need extra tutoring, some need responsibility. I can teach them a lot and I can arrange for them to work in other restaurants for short periods or, nowadays, they can join the Scottish Chefs Association (SCA) and go to educational dinners and training workshops. A lot of our staff joined as unskilled people straight from school. My head chef, Angus, came from school and he's been with us for 15 years. But we generally can't keep promising people. We expect them to leave, but we also expect them to discuss with us their ambitions and career expectations. We work with them to develop their talents. Sometimes I'm able to find them their next position with people I respect, that way they don't make a career mistake. Young people want to go from chef de partie to head chef in a matter of months, but you need maturity to run a kitchen, and you need to be even more mature to open your own restaurant."

Given his background, it's no surprise that David paid a great deal of attention to marketing. But he took a different approach from many other restaurateurs. Unusually for a restaurant, The Peat Inn has its own corporate identity. Until 1982, the restaurant marketing design was old peat carriers and a donkey. But with the major changes taking place, it was felt that a marketing revamp was required in keeping with the new look. The design needed to be light and modern and reflecting the fresh, open, unstuffy character of the restaurant. The Wilsons went to an Edinburgh design firm and gave them the brief of a modern design — something that combined food, a fork and the building. Between them, the designers and the Wilsons, came up with the concept of the building being on the end of a fork. The logo was doubly striking because most restaurants don't have a logo as such, usually they have a line drawing of the building or just use a typeface. They wanted the motif to be backed up with bright colours and came up with the idea of pink as the colour for letterhead paper and envelopes.

"We felt that the restaurant had to be a bit over-the-top, and that it had to reflect the fun of eating out", said David. "The success of our logo was measured by the same criteria as the logo of any other company. It could be put on all sorts of different pieces of merchandising and it worked."

The design motif, in itself quite outstanding, has been applied to a variety of merchandising, including a tie, a bottle of whisky, tabletop tortoises, sauce spoons and a jar of honey. The tie is individually painted and made of pure silk and comes either as a long tie or a bow-tie.

"We've sold hundreds of ties and made thousands of pounds. The merchandising is very profitable in business terms since it requires no additional in-house labour cost. We keep stocks low. But the merchandising articles are also talking points. People see them in the lounge and it gives them something to talk about."

David believed that the corporate identity approach has helped consolidate the restaurant in the marketplace. Since many of the restaurant customers are businessmen, they would be more appreciative of a quality corporate identity and feel, instinctively, that this was the right restaurant to bring their custom.

"Most restaurants have only two cost-effective methods of promoting their business", said David. "They can't usually afford a PR agency and they cannot control the ebb and flow of editorial coverage, if they are lucky enough to get any. But they can control the way they present themselves to existing or potential customers. In this respect, restaurants are like any other business.

• THE PEAT INN •

Selections from the Menu

Three Little Seafood Salads £10.50
Langoustine Broth with Langoustine Tails £8.50
Julienne of Pigeon Breast with Spiced Pork £9.00
Crispy Salmon Fillet with Chinese Spices £9.00
A Sauté of Scallops, Monkfish & Spiced Apple £9.00

Whole Lobster Poached in A Vegetable & Herb Broth £19.00
Roast Venison Saddle, Wild Mushroom and
Truffle Crust in a Red Wine Sauce £17.50
Roast Breast of Duck on Spiced Lentils £16.50

Caramelised Apple Pastry with a Caramel Sauce £6.00
A Trio of Caramel Desserts £6.00
A Feuilleté of White Chocolate Ice Cream
with a Dark Chocolate Sauce £6.00
Selection of Cheese £6.50

TASTING MENU £42.00
Warm Scallops and Langoustine with Herb Salad
Roast Halibut on Roast Vegetables with a Beef Juice
Julienne of Pigeon Breast on a Confit of Spiced Pork
Roast Venison Saddle, Wild Mushroom and
Truffle Crust in a Red Wine Sauce
Selection of Cheeses
Dessert from the A La Carte Menu
Coffee & Petits Fours

The most common tools are letter and telephone.

"We wanted to have a letterhead that would make people — whether they were journalists or businessmen, both of whom understood the value of quality design — sit up and take notice, that would make them look more closely at what we had to say because of the way the letter was presented.

"And with my background, I was able to write the copy for our brochure. Our brochure was very expensive to produce, because we wanted something distinctive, but again that has paid off in a very high response rate. We also use tent cards very effectively, leaving them in the lounge to promote aperitifs or our private room or The Residence.

"The telephone is an even more powerful tool if used correctly. I would advise chefs and restaurateurs to make effective use of the telephone their business priority. I'm not talking about making telephone calls out. I merely mean knowing how to answer the phone.

"Answering the telephone is our lifeline. Over 90 per cent of our business comes in via the telephone. So it is important to be able to deal with that properly. I am the person who answers the phone in The Peat Inn. If I'm elsewhere in the building, or at home, it will be my restaurant manager or the manager at The Residence. I answer the phone because I can give the customers the right answers. And I have the confidence. The last thing any restaurateur should do is delegate the telephone to a junior member of staff. I'll even break off cooking to answer the phone, even in the middle of service."

Over the past few years David has also been heavily involved in the Scottish Chefs Association, which was set up to train working chefs. He has been very excited by the response to the SCA — membership is now close to 500 — and especially by the SCA's initiative to open the Scottish Chefs Cookery School in the autumn of 1997. He believes it is important that the pioneering work done by a handful of Scottish chefs since the 1970s is carried forward by a larger band of young chef/entrepreneurs to help establish Scotland not just as a source of wonderful produce but also as a gastronomic destination.

David has been given an honorary degree of Doctor of Law (LLD) by Dundee University — probably the first Scottish chef to be recognised in this way. The Peat Inn has seen steady year-on-year growth apart from a period during the recession in the early 1990s. But restaurants are becoming more price sensitive. And recent growth has been maintained without increasing prices — there have been no price increases for three years. This has partly been achieved by using less expensive ingredients such as cod instead of turbot and items like venison liver and lamb shanks are particularly profitable. The culinary skills that goes into these dishes is no less than with more expensive ingredients.

But 1995 was a record year for the business and 1996 then set a new record. In November 1997, The Peat Inn will celebrate its silver anniversary, celebrating not just the culinary achievement of over two decades, but also the clear entrepreneurial skills whose flair was no more evident than when the Wilsons decided that there just had to be rooms at the inn.

PART TWO

General Caterers

GLASGOW'S TEAROOM QUEEN

• *Anne Mulhern at The Willow Tea Rooms* •

It will come as a great surprise to Anne Mulhern to be described as a typical entrepreneur. For she has no formal business qualifications, no business education, no business training, no accountancy skills, no marketing background. She doesn't even have much in the way of catering training. But she has two other priceless prerequisites — a small dream and stubbornness.

Long before the Charles Rennie Mackintosh boom, long before that marketing bandwagon took off, long before any 'real entrepreneur' with half a brain could see the value of a catering outlet themed around the architect, long before any of that, Anne was just a fan, a big fan. And like any fan, she was saddened by the lack of respect given to the architectural genius outside a small nucleus of devotees.

She was amazed to discover that original work by Mackintosh lay untouched and unseen in one of the city's busiest thoroughfares. In a stockroom above Hendersons the jewellers in Sauchiehall Street, the original Willow Tea Rooms lay in a state of neglect. But the room contained original Mackintosh doors, panels and windows. As a fan, she wanted to see the room restored to its original glory. But then, as a budding business person, she saw an opportunity.

Strange though it may seem, Glasgow invented the tea room (or tea shop, as it was known in England). Stuart Cranston, a tea dealer, opened the country's first tea room in 1875 at No 2 Queen Street. Four years before, he had set up shop in St Enoch Square as a tea retailer — at a time when Glasgow rivalled London as a centre of tea blending with 160 tea dealers listed in directories — and such was his commitment that he kept a kettle to hand so that he could offer customers sample cups. When he moved to Queen Street, it occurred to him to charge for the sample cups, and so he set up tables where customers could sit and drink tea for tuppence a cup with bread and cakes extra.

Tea rooms owe their popularity to the strength of the Temperance movement, to the Scottish style of sweet baking and to the traditional high tea. But the first tearoom was not, as it was later to become, the meeting place for fine ladies in fine hats. The first tearoom was a meeting place for businessmen.

But it was Stuart's sister Kate, the legendary Miss Cranston (although her married name was Cochrane), who raised the tearoom to its elevated heights. She opened her first establishment in 1878 in Argyle Street. But eight years later, when she opened her second tearoom in Ingram Street, the unique Cranston style, with its commitment to progressive interior design, was beginning to show. Her Buchanan Street Tea Rooms in 1896 was markedly bolder in style and introduced work by Mackintosh for the first time. A year later, in her new Argyle Street premises, the famous Mackintosh high-backed chairs made their debut.

The Mackintosh-Cranston tour de force was the opening of the Willow Tea Rooms in Sauchiehall Street in November 1903. On the ground floor was a tea room at the front and a lunch room at the back. On a mezzanine floor was the Tea Gallery and on the first floor was the Room De Luxe with billiard and smoke rooms on the second floor. The Room De Luxe was extravagant and sumptuous with a long bay window overlooking the street, set with a design in mirror glass, and around the room was a frieze of leaded mirror panels and a pair of glittering doors. It cost an extra penny a cup to sit in this room.

But within a quarter of a century, the Willow Tea Rooms had been sold to the neighbouring department store which turned the premises over to retail use and over the next 50 years Glasgow gradually ran out of tearooms. When Daly's left the premises in 1978, the new owners undertook to restore the building as much as possible to the original design. Hendersons took over the premises to operate as a jeweller's store on the ground floor with the mezzanine used for display purposes. The first floor — home to the Room De Luxe — was converted into a stockroom.

A few years later came the 26-year-old Anne Mulhern with the idea of renting out the stockroom and turning it back, as much as was commercially possible, into the Willow Tea Rooms. There wasn't much in Anne's background to suggest that she was the person to take on such an ambitious project. She was born in Glasgow in 1956 and lived in Carntyne, in the city's east end. Her father was an engineer. On leaving school, she worked for nine years as a clerk in the WD & HO Wills cigarette factory. During this time, she took a City & Guilds catering course at Glasgow College of Food Technology for six months. But her only experience in the catering business was a short stint at Maestro's in Scott Street and a part-time waiting position in Woodies Bar in the Holiday Inn Hotel.

"But I wanted to do something for myself", said Anne. "I was probably so persistent because I really didn't think the idea would become a reality. I wasn't a business person. I had no real experience. But I was saddened at the thought of the Willow Tea Rooms going to waste and perhaps that was what kept me fired up. I thought that if I was successful, that in itself would be my reward. I would have achieved an ambition."

She approached Mr Henderson about her idea and gradually he gave in to her persistence. She drew up a business plan and applied to the Scottish Development Agency (the forerunner of Scottish Enterprise) for a loan and received £10,000 under the Small Loans Guarantee Scheme which loaned money at 3 per cent over the base rate, but had the psychological safety net that 90 per cent of the loan was guaranteed if the business failed.

Anne invested £5,000 of her own money, and the bulk of the cash went on replica Mackintosh furniture and a cappuccino machine. The Mackintosh chair designs were copied from pictures in a book by a company in Bridge of Allan. And, of course, there was no need to spend on any other decor since the original window, panels and doors were still there.

She enrolled her tutor at the college as development chef to help her design a simple menu. There were considerable restrictions on what could be offered on the menu. Because it was a listed building, she was prevented from having a proper cooker and, therefore, from having cooking on the premises, other than toasting and dishes reheated by microwave. Her kitchen equipment consisted of a toaster, three microwaves, a dishwasher and a processor to do the grating and slicing. Rather than give in to this, Anne decided she would make soup and chilli on her domestic cooker at home at night and on Sunday and transport them in her car. She bought in the baked products.

Meanwhile, she researched tearooms, looking at operational systems and design and menus. Deciding on pricing was her first real business decision, and perhaps indicative of her growing confidence. She decided — as Miss Cranston had done 80 years before — that she could afford to charge a little bit more than the going rate for the privilege of people eating in such distinguished, historic and unusual surroundings. Her second real business decision was to find a way of bringing the opening to the attention of the public. Despite her own diffidence, and without any connections at all in the media, and with only an inkling of the worth of the project, she invited Lord Provost Michael Kelly to open the new tearoom.

The 44-seater Willow Tea Rooms opened in 1983 with a menu consisting of three types of tea, cappuccino, toasted sandwiches, soup, chilli con carne, quiche and pancakes, crumpets and scones. The Lord Provost's opening was performed the day before and featured in both Glasgow main newspapers, the *Herald* and the *Evening Times*.

The result was a queue on the first day and the operation maintained a steady level of growth, with daily business now at 200-300 covers. The tearoom received an enormous boost with the opening of the Mackintosh Exhibition almost across the road in the McLellan Galleries — creating queues every day — and the exhibition's subsequent tour in America has generated tremendous tourist interest.

The tearoom opens from 9.30am to 4.30pm Monday to Saturday. There is no cover charge and no minimum charge and virtually no other restriction so that customers can simply have a cup of tea at lunchtime or afternoon tea in the morning or breakfast in the afternoon. "People were asking for breakfast at lunchtime and mid-afternoon so we decided the customer must be right", said Anne.

Perhaps as a result of the restrictions on cooking on the premises, Anne was forced into having a simpler menu than she might have originally have attempted. But this proved beneficial, as she did not fall into the trap of menu overload which bedevils so many fledgling operations. The menu did grow and substantially, but the core menu remained the same so that operationally it was simple to handle. Now there are a 27 different teas on offer including Keemun, Rose Petal, fruit teas, herbal teas and her own blend which can be adjusted to suit personal preferences. There are 13 varieties of coffee as well as soft drinks. There is an all-day breakfast to suit different nationalities from traditional British to pancakes & maple syrup and French toast & strawberries. And there are sandwiches, toasties, baked potatoes, filled croissants and bagels, and salads. Main meals range from haggis, neeps & tatties to Scottish smoked salmon cornets and Arbroath smokie. Afternoon tea includes, sandwiches, scones with butter, jam and cream, cakes and pastries and tea or coffee.

• WILLOW TEA ROOMS •

Selections from the Menu

Pot of Tea £1.30 • Glass of Lemon Tea £1.10
Pot of Fruit Tea £1.30 • Pot of Herbal Tea £1.30
Cappuccino £1.30 • Cappuccino with Marshmallow £1.45
Espresso £1.30 • Cafetiere of Coffee £1.75
Hot Chocolate £1.40
Pepsi £1.00 • Mineral Water £1.50
Fresh Orange Juice £1.20
Ice Cream Milk Shake £1.50
Home-Made Soup £2.10
Prawns in Tomato Mayonnaise £2.45
Tuna Mayonnaise Sandwich £3.45
Hand-Carved Roast Ham & Cheddar Cheese Toastie £3.75
Baked Potato with Haggis Filling served with Salad £3.95
Smoked Salmon with Cream Cheese Bagel/Croissant £4.95
Hot Roast Beef with Potatoes and Vegetables £5.50
Haggis, Neeps & Tatties £4.50
Scottish Smoked Salmon & Scrambled Eggs £4.95
Soused Herring with Baked Potato £4.65
Selection of Salads £4.95
Scrambled Eggs with Potato Scone & Ayrshire Bacon £4.25
French Toast with Strawberries £3.50
Pancakes & Maple Syrup £2.75
Toasts & Tea-Breads with Jam £1.20 - £1.70
Caramel Shortcake £1.35
Carrot Cake £1.75 • Apple Tart £1.95
Meringues with Strawberries & Fresh Cream £1.95
Strawberry Sundae £2.65
Afternoon Tea £7.25

She still does all the soups and hot cooked main courses at home, although with experience this takes a lot less time. In fact, since the tearoom closes in the late afternoon, it's simply a case of working on for another couple of hours cooking at home. She has improved her cooking skills and cooks hams and chickens and other main courses at home. She recently added home-made meringues, served with cream, for £1.75 to her domestic repertoire and since they have that big, home-made look about them, are selling extremely well and, of course, are very profitable.

She has developed her culinary range, helped enormously by attending an eight-day cookery course for beginners run last summer by the Scottish Chefs Association, where she also acquired presentation skills. Average spend is around £4.00 and the tea room serves 200-300 covers a day and turnover has more than doubled since she spent £70,000 opening the 54-seat mezzanine area as an additional tea room, bringing the total seating capacity to 102. Turnover has shot up since 1985 when revenues totalled around £70,000. For 1996, turnover reached over £330,000 — an amazing 123 per cent rise over the previous year.

Her entrepreneurial instincts have been sharpened by forays into merchandising which now generates about £20,000 a year and is very cost effective since it requires no extra labour cost. She began introducing merchandising two years when customers started to ask for mementoes of their visit. Initially, she only produced postcards which sold for 95p, but now the range of goods is considerably more extensive. This includes Willow Tea Rooms own blend of tea in Willow fabric bags, and the bag itself can be sold separately. She has produced a specially commissioned tea caddie featuring the tea rooms and filled with tea as well as bone china mugs, ceramic carrier bags, and a range of jams, preserves, chutneys and confectionery. She also sells an exclusive range of prints depicting the exterior of the building and the interior of the Room De Luxe by Glasgow artist Tom Gardner as well as mounted and framed photographs.

The opening of the mezzanine spurred her to tackle marketing more seriously. But she had a small budget of only £3,000. She opened the refurbished room on St Valentine's Day and garnered considerable press coverage. But it was making a positive link with the Rennie Mackintosh exhibition (which attracted 250,000 visitors) that produced outstanding results. Anticipating a high level of interest in the exhibition, she compiled a PR and direct mail database and sent a press pack to every UK design and architectural magazine including such prestigious titles as *International Vogue* and *Homes & Gardens*. Each press pack also contained a full set of Willow Tea Room postcards and information on the Mackintosh Festival. She also offered her premises as a free location backdrop to magazine photographers on the understanding that they would give her a mention. The response to this offer was phenomenal.

She also wrote to all bed and breakfasts in the area and asked them to send their guests to the tea rooms. All her staff, including herself, were sent on training courses, and as a result of attending the Scottish Chefs Association training course she had the confidence to put more Scottish dishes on the menu. The merchandising was developed to capitalise on the event, and was so successful that she ended up selling her products to other retailers.

She also discovered that the McLellan Galleries which was hosting the Mackintosh Exhibition was not offering visitors catering facilities so she was able to promote directly to visitors.

The marketing initiatives increased sales in the first six months by 112 per cent and grew profits by 104 per cent. The campaign was so successful that it won the Small Business Marketing Award in the annual Scottish Thistle Awards.

The award itself generated further publicity, proof, if any were needed, that here was a true entrepreneur at work. And like any good entrepreneur, Anne did not stop there. With the business developing so well, Anne decided to see if the same concept would work elsewhere and in spring 1997 started looking around for new premises in Glasgow city centre. In some respects, she was taking on not just the Mackintosh mantle but the business route of Kate Cranston. For Cranston had set out to own more than one tea shop and now Ann Mulhern decided to go the same way. She purchased a three-storey building at the bottom of Buchanan Street across from the Princes Square shopping mall.

The new venture, which opened in summer 1997, was named Willow Tea Rooms Buchanan Street. The property provides 120-seats over two floors with another floor available for offices and training and possibly a Mackintosh exhibition space. Each of the seating areas are themed after other famous Mackintosh restaurants, the White Room in Ingram Street which was designed in 1900 and the Chinese (or Blue) Room also in Ingram Street which was designed in 1911.

Unlike Sauchiehall Street, the new operation will have its own purpose-built kitchen. The menu will follow similar lines to Sauchiehall Street. The new restaurant will have 22 full and part-time staff. Anne will oversee the operation with each restaurant having its own manager.

It's often said that you need vision to become an entrepreneur. If that's the case, then Anne Mulhern is a classic example. Why had nobody else thought to do what she has done? By the same token, why did she have that spark of initiative?

Those are questions which might never be answered. What we do know is that without the efforts of Anne Mulhern, the Willow Tea Rooms would never have been revived and become a tourist attraction in their own right.

TREASURE OF THE NORTH

• *The Gosden & Wilkie Families at The Clifton* •

Catering in Scotland is full of family businesses. Families run hotels, restaurants, guesthouses, cafés, and tearooms. They often make a great deal of this fact in their promotional literature as if it was some kind of kitemark or mark of excellence. But a family-run business in Scotland is the least likely to survive for more than one generation.

There are many reasons for this, some of which the catering industry shares with every other type of business. Permutate any of the following: businesses, in general, have a hard time keeping going for a decade never mind a lifetime; youngsters are often put off going into the parental business simply by being forced to work in the business from an early age; the potential successors clearly lack the required business skills; families often don't want their children to follow them; and the business isn't big enough to support an extended family involvement or to expand to make it possible.

The catering business has other reasons for falling into the yawning generation gap. Often catering outlets, especially hotels and restaurants, are purchased as an investment for retirement so family succession is out of the question. Operations are run for the wrong reasons, by people who always 'dreamed' of their own restaurant or guesthouse and are almost never in a fit state to be properly profitable. Families often live on or above the premises and youngsters are put off by never being able to escape the business. Bracket any of the above with the fact that there is a very high mortality rate in the catering business anyway and it's no surprise that few businesses get the opportunity to be passed on to a second generation.

So the Wilkie/Gosden families are unusual. For The Clifton, at Tyndrum, is now in its third generation of family management. The Clifton itself is pretty rare. It's hard to describe exactly what it is, but if you're on the way to Oban or Fort William you can't miss it. It's most commonly described as a mini-service station, but that removes entirely the sense of charm and originality that pervades the operation. It comprises a 220-seater restaurant, a craft shop, food and gift shop, whisky shop, sandwich take-away, bureau de change, a country clothing shop and a petrol station.

It was born in 1965 as a much smaller enterprise altogether — consisting of a general store, post office, delivery van, petrol pump and house. It was bought as a family business by 52-year-old Leslie and Betty Gosden and their 19-year-old son Lamond and daughter Lesley and Lesley's 26-year-old husband Derek Wilkie. Leslie Gosden, born in England, had been a businessman in Edinburgh. Derek Wilkie was an open cast mining engineer who had just returned from Nigeria with his wife.

They came to Tyndrum at a time when car travelling was going through its first major boom and roadside cafés were springing up all over the country. Many of these eateries were on major trunk roads, in the days when trunk roads were still on scenic routes, and while some of the operations were close to a petrol station or a shop, few businesses consisted of more than a restaurant or what was no more than an dressed-up transport café. Invariably, they were single-unit businesses in independent hands. Since this was long before the era of frozen or pre-prepared meals or production kitchens, food, of a fairly simple variety, was produced on the premises.

It was Lord Forte who hit upon the idea of a brand of roadside restaurants when he created the Little Chef operation. The expansion of the motorway network in the sixties, seventies and eighties was actually what made possible the kind of roadside service station common today. Without the motorways, without the ease of transport that made far-off areas accessible as long as they were on or close by a motorway, it would have been impossible to deliver the frozen food or pre-prepared meals that dominate the sector today.

The Clifton business was a good site for a general business because of its location. The addition of a 24-seater restaurant soon after the Wilkie/Gosden family took over was the first indication that it had the potential to be a great site. Tyndrum is a tiny village on the main road north just after Crianlarich. The road was the scenic link between two great tourist attractions, the Trossachs just to the south and the west coast to the north. Tyndrum could almost be described as a staging post for anyone heading one way along the A85 towards Oban and the ferry to Mull and the islands or the other way along the A82 to Glencoe and Fort William and thence to Mallaig or the Kyle of Lochalsh or to Inverness.

And it was also clear that the Trossachs themselves would prevent the creation of a motorway system north that could bypass Tyndrum and destroy the tourist traffic in the way that many years later the building of the A82 bypassing Balloch at the foot of Loch Lomond changed forever that little tourist town.

With the motorway threat removed, then conversely almost anything that happened to the roads could only strengthen the opportunity for the Clifton. There was no likelihood of an alternative route north. But road widening and other improvements could only encourage greater road traffic. Oddly enough, some road restrictions could work in favour of a place like the Clifton. Tyndrum is pretty much pure relief for any driver who has battled along the A82 at its most devilish from Tarbet to Crianlarich with a tortuous winding road compressed by sheer rock on one side and Loch Lomond on the other and most likely stuck behind a caravan or lorry with any ideas of overtaking nothing but suicidal impulse. When they get to the end what most drivers want to do is stop. Crianlarich is the first option, but drivers come upon it too quickly and the houses are piled close to the road and by the time you turn under the bridge you are almost leaving, the village is gone before you know it, and unless you know where you are headed, it's not easy to stop. Tyndrum is a more attractive prospect. The approach road is wide and straight and you see the village long before you arrive.

Tyndrum was established as a resting and grazing place during the great cattle droves of the seventeenth to nineteenth centuries. Lead and silver were produced in mines in the area for two centuries until the twenties and production of gold in economic quantities is due to begin. And the Tyndrum/Crianlarich area had been a 'cross roads' for both road and rail travel.

But scenery was the main attraction. Scenery, wherever it was on the west coast, was beginning to exert a profitable fascination for coach tour operators. Companies like Wallace Arnold were beginning to recognise the potential for not just day-tripping tourists, but also short-break tours and were always on the lookout for interesting places, preferably outside the congestion of a town, where they could take a meal or snack break.

So in 1974, the Clifton decided to give tourists a better reason to stop. The challenge was to turn a casual restaurant-stop into a must-stop destination.

The idea was to give the village the shopping and catering facilities of a town.

A major expansion programme increased the seating capacity of the restaurant tenfold — to its current 220 seats — the food shop and the craft shop. A larger restaurant would have been a good investment in itself, but already the owners had realised that tourists, having decided to stop anyway, might be willing to spend more on things other than food.

The small business became a much larger business, a more obvious business, physically more dominating as a building, and yet with no vulgar signage, so that people were inclined to 'discover' it in an enthusiastic manner, the best promotional tool for tourist businesses. Its name, the Clifton Coffee House and Craft Centre, did not quite do it justice, but then something more ostentatious might have put people off.

The risk was twofold. For a restaurant to go from 24 seats to 220 seats is a colossal gamble in any language. But in many respects, the two families were responding to demand. Food in the smaller operation had to be very limited. But the larger operation could be custom-built with a stronger menu. The operation also meant a major increase in catering staff. But they were not looking for such skilled labour. The cooking was going to be home-made, so it was more a question of organisation.

The bigger risk was in the retail expansion. For the petrol and catering business had very good cash-flow with relatively little tied up in stock for any period of time. However, a gift shop would have a good deal tied up in stock for a considerably longer period.

Even so, if the restaurant worked, the increased cash flow could carry the shop over the initial period. And it did work.

For a decade or so, the Clifton Coffee House and Craft Centre sat quite easily within the roadside-service-station sector, if a cut above the rest. But the addition of The Green Welly Shop country clothing store in 1987 signalled a change. This had its origins in a small accessory counter in the petrol station. The counter was intended to only sell wellington boots and mackintoshes, but the customers kept asking for other items. The boom in outdoor activity and with so much of it taking place on The Clifton's doorstep seemed too good an opportunity to miss.

It was anticipated that people would spend more time in the clothing store than the gift shop and that the centre would, therefore, as a whole, attract more than just the passer-by. To some extent, this policy has worked, the clothing store successful in its own right, but it has generally been seen by the public as a separate operation. Because the Green Welly Shop has a separate entrance, with no corridor linking it to The Clifton, the public often thinks there is no connection at all. But the addition of The Green Welly Shop gave The Clifton more in common with a department store than a service station.

While service stations do have gift shops, they do not sell the quality of product to be found in The Clifton and are more likely to concentrate on books, small toys, magazines, biscuits and compact discs. Service stations have also undergone a dramatic shift in catering terms. From the mid-eighties onwards the bulk of food sold was pre-packaged. In the nineties, much of the food operation was franchised out to established chain-food operations like McDonalds, Burger King and Harry Ramsdens.

The Clifton has worked in the opposite direction, aiming to consolidate and improve its original features and to add new ideas that would give the operation a fresh appeal while remaining within the initial philosophy.

The main area was re-designed and refurbished three years ago. A sandwich take-away was added at the entranceway last year, but the sandwiches are the same as those sold in the restaurant. Home-made fudge and Nardinis ice-cream was also introduced in this area.

The Clifton is a tourist centre and dependent on the unpredictable tourist trade. But it attracts over 300,000 visitors a year, of whom about 65 per cent are coach trade although private car customers spend more. With more than 4,500 coaches arriving mostly unannounced — few book — the restaurant has been designed for fast customer flow. A recent audit showed that customers come from all over the world including considerable numbers of French, German and Dutch tourists.

The centre opens from 8.30am until 5.30pm and the petrol station stays open longer till 10.00pm. It used to close in January and February for refurbishment but in 1996, for the first time, successfully remained open during that period.

The restaurant is the most profitable part of the business and petrol the least profitable. The craft shop is next best profitable, followed by clothing, food and whisky. Customers stop for food, fuel and the toilets. Some customers just use the restaurant, others come every day. The restaurant takes up the largest space and is on two levels. A great deal of thought has gone into the design to ease customer flow, facilitate clearing-up and reduce noise levels.

Seating is unusual. This is effectively a series of rectangular booths around rectangular fixed tables with the aisles kept clear of seating. But it works and allows staff to clear tables more easily. Fixed seating eliminates the noise of scraping chairs which could easily turn into an unbearable cacophony of noise in such a confined area. The floor is covered with linatol to reduce noise levels. Trolleys staff use for clearing tables also have rubber wheels to keep the noise down.

Service is speedy, devised in such a way as to ensure that coachloads could get served quickly. The food is self-service but hot dishes are ordered at the counter and brought to the table by counter staff.

There are four main kitchen areas — bakery, salads, hot meals and sandwiches. The bakery produces 38,000 scones and 2,000 traybakes a year. The wash-up is contained within the bakery area and crockery can be rotated as often as eight times a day. The sandwich section makes anything from 20-40 dozen sandwiches daily working to a production system with sandwiches put in plastic containers, labelled and priced. This section supplies the petrol station and take-away.

Everything on the extensive menu of meals and snacks is home-made. The average spend is £1.50 in the morning and £5.00-6.50 at lunch. There are hot meals, salads, soups, sandwiches, cakes, desserts and beverages. No chips are sold because of the smell, and there's no ice-cream in the restaurant either for space reasons.

The take-away section at the entrance to the centre was introduced to cater for people who want fed but don't want to eat in the restaurant. A display counter sells sandwiches and snacks. Home-made fudge has become a big part of the business, along with ice-cream and liquor tastings. Customers can watch the fudge being made and they can sample the product.

The business employs 60 staff, few of whom are part-time. Staff work full-time during the season till October, then on short time in the off-season. Opening longer would mean finding more staff, but Tyndrum itself is a tiny village and only supplies 20 per cent of the staff. The rest come from further afield and the company operates a mini-bus to bring them to and from work.

This is the operation that the next generation of Wilkies, siblings Iain Wilkie and Fiona Robertson, will inherit. They are the grandchildren of the founder. From the age of 11, they attended boarding school at Morrison's Academy, 40 miles away in Crieff. And unlike their parents and grandparents, both have gone to catering college and have extensive catering experience outside the family.

Fiona had the option of doing a physical education degree or one involving catering. She chose to study hotel and catering management at Napier College in Edinburgh. On graduation, she worked in food and beverage with Sheraton Hotels. Then she moved to the Mount Charlotte Thistle Hotel Group in Aberdeen where, first of all, she managed a brasserie operation and then was asked to set up and manage a room service system. She rounded off her catering skills by running a large Safeway customer restaurant in Aberdeen before returning to the Clifton in 1983. By this time, the original partnership had broken up, Leslie and Derek Gosden having gone into retirement, leaving Derek and Lesley Wilkie and Lamond Gosden in charge.

Iain also went to Napier College, but spent most of his career in the Far East, firstly with the Hong Kong Hilton and then as food and beverage co-ordinator for the new Shanghai Hilton. He joined the Clifton in 1988.

"I grew up with the business and loved it", said Fiona. "I was clearing tables at the age of nine. It was a good way to earn extra pocket money. Because we were sent away to boarding school when my parents were building up the business, The Clifton did not come to dominate our lives. I only saw my father during the holidays, but we had the chance to see The Clifton objectively, from the outside, and we could see that it was actually a good business. I always knew I wanted to come back, I wasn't blackmailed into it."

Added Iain, "Working in the Far East was a single person's life. I was ready to come home, and I came in to this small family-run business with my high-flying catering background to work with my father and mother who had no formal training. I was bursting with ideas and inevitably I ran into a brick wall."

"At that stage, we were both employees, we were not partners", said Fiona.

There were inevitable clashes and a period of learning on both sides, especially about ways of communicating how to introduce change. Ian and Fiona wanted more formal structures, so that problems could be more easily identified. They realised that gradual change was the way forward backed up by good reason. Because of their training, they were able to look at every aspect of the restaurant business and seek out improvements. They were both employed as hands-on managers rather than executives.

"We actually know a great deal about our business", said Fiona. "We know what the computers tell us, but we are also able to act on observation and experience. The computer may tell us that we sell more tea than coffee, but we observe that walkers and climbers tend to buy mugs and foreigners buy cappuccino. And because the computer tells us that sticky toffee pudding and boozy bread-and-butter pudding are our best-selling desserts, we look to see how we can use that information. Can we increase dessert sales if we put on similar items?"

"We don't let our training get the better of us either", commented Iain. "It seems more sensible, for example, to sell our fudge in pre-packed containers but customers don't want to buy it that way. They want to see it weighed out. It's more footery for our staff to do it that way, but it's what the customer wants, it's the way it's best sold. Equally, we are always looking for sensible efficiencies. Bread which has been buttered for sandwiches but not used is used later for bread-and-butter pudding. Our clearing staff are told to salvage unused milk portions and sugar sachets. We serve tea from a big pot because it's more aesthetically pleasing and tastes better than if it's come from a tea urn, but the teapot is especially wide and has handles to make it lift more easily."

"People thought we would come in with wide-sweeping general changes", added Fiona. "But in point of fact, good catering is about detail. And that attention to detail applies to staff as well as product or equipment. We want to make the system work better. For example, staff on the service counter swap positions every 30 minutes to avoid stress. And we let the staff have their lunch at lunchtime rather than before as is common with most restaurants.

"But some of our problems seem insoluble no matter how big we get. Because of our location, we can't get daily deliveries of fresh produce. Our meat, for example, arrives fresh but we have to freeze it. For our soups and stews, we use fresh vegetables backed up by frozen due to the sheer volume produced — on a busy day we use 180 litres of home-made soup.

"But we must be doing something right, because our level of business in the restaurant has increased substantially over the last eight years."

The most important single reason why most family businesses fail is the reason they came together in the first place. A family is not a business structure and it is almost impossible to run a business using the family as a model. Companies which say they treat employees as members of their family tend to forget the fact that deploying a patronising or benevolent approach is far removed from becoming embroiled in the real emotional traumas, real or imagined, which beset family life.

Family businesses are often like dysfunctional families. There are many ways for family businesses, just like families, to fail. Even if there is a structure, members feel empowered to tear it up at any moment if they disagree with a decision. In the heat of the moment it is hard to maintain respect for a business manager who is a close relative. Aspects of business failure, like old wounds in a family, are re-opened at the drop of a hat. Families living too much in each other's pockets often fail as families and more so when there is the added pressure of keeping a business afloat. Families without a proper business training usually lack a long-term outlook and rip out the profits as soon as possible.

But as many family businesses fail because people do not speak up as because of violent disagreement. The alternative to managers indulging in messy familial emotions in their business is for families to be so pointedly averse to causing a disturbance that they avoid business discussion altogether.

Should family businesses survive long enough to be handed down, another vexed question raises its ugly head. How much does the retiring — and usually founding — manager take out of the business. If the business was just sold straightforwardly to a third party, there would be no problem. But for a business to continue trading profitably, the last thing it needs is a partner demanding to be paid off or for the inheritance to turn into a burden by the inheritor having to raise substantial sums to take on the business.

The Clifton was an unusual family business in that it was begun by two generations together, rather than by one generation which then brought their offspring into the business. Although Leslie and Betty Gosden were the elder generation, they were in their sixties by the time the real decisions about the development of the business were being taken. It was the younger generation, Derek and Lesley Wilkie and Lamond Gosden who were the driving force behind the major growth in 1974.

But the age differences between the generations created conflict. The older couple, looking to their retirement, wanted a no-risk development. The more ambitious younger generation was willing to risk more. The ownership transition to the second generation was very painful and almost destroyed the business. When Leslie and Betty Gosden retired in the late seventies, they were convinced that the gamble would not work and that the business would not survive. Consequently, when they retired, they took a lot more out of the business than was healthy for the business.

The second generation ran the business by each taking individual responsibility for a section of the operation. Lamond was in charge of the food and gift shop. Lesley was in control of the restaurant and Craft Shop and Derek ran the Green Welly Shop as well as acting as manager of the overall business. The trio worked well together, especially as they were allowed autonomy within their own units.

However, by the time the third generation arrived, with their new ideas, the business was far bigger than when this simple structure had been devised. However, Iain and Fiona were taken on as employees first of all, not partners, with no share in the profits. Like any employee, they had to prove their worth. Equally, their parents were determined to avoid the messy transition they had to endure.

In due course, Iain took over the general managership. Fiona manages the restaurant. Lamond continues to oversee part of the retail operation. Edward, Fiona's husband, manages the specialist Whisky Shop and the foyer operation. Derek provides general back-up where and when required. Lesley is in the main retired but is more than happy to maintain the small frontal garden and then provide help in training. Senior members of staff (some with over 20 years service) are still in key positions but planning for future years will be around young, enthusiastic managers now in place within the business.

The partnership issue has also been resolved. Derek has passed the bulk of his shares to Iain and Lesley is in the throes of handing over to Fiona. Lamond, who has the largest remaining share, will be making a move in the near future to reduce his interest down a similar route. Indeed, the planning for family succession is almost complete.

"It was important that we serve an apprenticeship", said Fiona. "We needed to find out if we could all work together and at the end of the day still remain a family. Iain and I work together but choose not to socialise."

"Over the last few years", said Ian, "we probably had, for the first time, a real management structure, rather than everyone doing their own thing without any questions asked. We are just beginning to see the benefits of a more cohesive management structure, both in terms of day-to-day management and in terms of developing a longer-term strategy. The Clifton had been labouring under having too few managers, not the usual problem of too many. Hands-on management had worked well for many years, but its was time to change. We still all have our own areas of responsibility, but we pull together more as a team and we have a clearer management policy."

"One of the problems", said Fiona, "was that we had no breathing space. All we had time for was doing the job. There was no time for staff training or for standing back and taking a hard look at the way the business was run. We

• THE CLIFTON •

Selections from the Menu

Full Breakfast Plate
Hot Bacon Roll
Freshly Baked Croissants
Carrot Cake
Gingerbread
Fruit Loaves
Banana Loaf

Cock-a-Leekie Soup
Curried Parsnip & Apple Soup
Cullen Skink

Smoked Salmon Sandwich/Roll
Mushroom & Leek Salad
Lasagne
Chilli
Vegetarian Pasta
Hebridean Leek Pie
Highland Steak Mince
Rabbit Casserole
Chicken Curry
Home-Made Farmhouse Pie
Home-Made Spicy Pork & Bean Pie
Baked Potatoes
Burgers

Sticky Toffee Pudding
Boozy Bread & Butter Pudding
Eve's Pudding
Home-Made Trifle
Home-Made Apple Pie

started out easing our staff into positions of more responsibility by appointing team leaders who were authorised to take decisions rather than leaving every decision, no matter how small, to one of the family.

"At the beginning of 1996 we bit the bullet and gave the team leaders proper managerial positions. That in turn led to the creation of under-managers or deputy managers. Because there was so much input in the past from family members, there had never been any onus of the actual staff to come up with ideas to develop their individual part of the business. The appointment of managers and deputies in itself allowed us to develop a real management structure. Passing more responsibility down the line also freed up management time at the top. Our overall general manager is more like a hotel general manager who can step into any department and act as a sounding board to help identify and sort out problems."

With a sound management structure in place, the company was able to tighten up various areas of operation and deal effectively with long-standing areas of concern. And relieved of the need to become involved in so many mundane matters, the top management team is able to devote more attention to strategic development. Despite its success, The Clifton has very much been in the catch-up business, expanding to meet demand. The only business where the company was in the vanguard of anticipated consumer demand was in the opening of the Green Welly Shop. But even that has a limited product range, being devoted entirely to general outdoor activity and does not stock any products relating to fishing or skiing.

The first area to benefit from a clearer company outlook has been in marketing. The old name of Clifton Coffee House and Craft Shop was in use right up until the end of 1995, even though it misled the public as to the size and range of the catering operation and took no account of the Green Welly Shop. It was decided to rebrand the entire operation as The Clifton and to design a brochure that would support this utilising the corporate identity with a Gaelic symbol that had been in place since 1980. In the brochure this was applied to each individual operation in a different colour. The decision to go for a 12-page brochure was based on the need for plenty of space to explain all the attractions on offer. The Clifton name preceded each individual unit, so that overall the operation was known as The Clifton and inside the customer could visit The Clifton Whisky Shop and The Clifton Restaurant etc. The brochure also had a wide distribution to tourist information centres, tour operators, hotels and customers.

The revamped marketing campaign has had an immediate effect. The clearer branding has made the public more aware of The Clifton's existence. Tour operators have also responded positively. The management team are convinced that the new brochure and clear branding has been the major reason for the substantial upturn in business in 1996. The company was projecting seven per cent growth on the restaurant side, but the increase has been more in the order of 18-20 per cent for the year to date, with August a record 30 per cent up on the previous year.

"Because we are more organised, we are more focused", said Fiona. "And because we are more focused, we know exactly what we are, and we are much more confident in getting our message across.

"And just as important to us is that we have come through a period of considerable change and we are all still family."

A RESTAURANT WITHOUT SEATS

• Suzanne Ritchie at Mise En Place •

For most of the eighties Suzanne Ritchie had been cultivating a pedigree as the welcoming, efficient persona fronting some of Glasgow's most prestigious restaurants such as The Buttery, One Devonshire Gardens and The Triangle as well as Brian Turner's new London restaurant.

But when she started her own outside catering business, Mise en Place, in October 1990 in her two-bedroom flat on Glasgow's south side, the pedigree appeared next to useless. She was driven by the desire to own and manage her own business after more than a decade of nurturing businesses she did not own. And she was gambling on somewhat rusty culinary skills and what she perceived to be a gap in the market. Four years later, the gamble led her to identify an even bigger gap and, inevitably, an even bigger risk.

Private catering is one of the unsung parts of the catering industry. It is undertaken by some very large firms, but mostly by very small ones. You need very little in the way of premises, a domestic cooker will do nicely, and often you can get away without much actual cooking, sandwiches and salads do nicely too. Many such small businesses are only part-time, providing small returns for small effort.

Private catering really took off during the recession as companies realised they could no longer afford to go to a hotel every time they needed to hold a seminar or meeting or a client lunch. It was cheaper to call in an outside caterer and have the food come to the company rather than the company go to the food. It was also easier; the outside caterers made all the running, they treated you like a real client rather than just another customer, they seemed to really want the business. And it had always seemed strange to the business community which spent all its time chasing orders, really pushing for business, to spend so much of its entertainment budget in restaurants which never seemed to pursue business at all.

The private catering market grew and in a very diverse way. Some companies went the whole way and became contract caterers, working in kitchens in their clients premises. Other companies started off making and delivering sandwiches and ended up making and delivering sandwiches. In between, there were a host of companies who did a wide range of catering from weddings, funerals, anniversaries, buffets, barbecues and private parties to marquees, sporting events and event management.

But one of the great beauties of private or outside catering was that it could be kept small, that all the costs that sometimes seemed so uncontrollable to hotels and restaurants could be kept under control. For example, there was very little waste because orders were taken in advance and the caterer need only buy in exactly what was required. By the same token, the caterer did not have to prepare ten or twenty different dishes, as a restaurant would, for with outside catering the customer, while offered choice, makes up his mind in advance. And so, on the day, the caterer need only be concerned with preparing the dishes ordered and not all the meals on the menu. Labour costs could be held down because again the caterer knew in advance exactly what staffing was required. And the caterer did not need to invest in an expensive restaurant as a showcase for his culinary wares, nor worry about the overhead when that showcase was empty.

Since the customer never saw the preparation or cooking premises, it did not matter where the food was cooked, as long as it met the hygiene and environmental health regulations. And so a great many such businesses could begin in a domestic kitchen, and expand when necessary.

Suzanne Ritchie began in just this way, on a four-ring Zanussi domestic cooker with a single oven in her flat in Pollokshields. It was the result of a conversation with a friend who was a director of Maclay Murray & Spens, the solicitors. The friend had been complaining about the quality of the twice-weekly lunches supplied by an outside caterer. Suzanne thought she could do better.

She offered a two-course restaurant-style lunch of fresh fish pie and lemon soufflé for 12 people, bought in the supplies from her local supermarket, turned her kitchen into a battle zone, delivered the dishes in the back of her Peugeot 205, served the meal using the company's plates and crockery and held her breath. At the end of the meal she was asked to repeat the lunch the next week and also deliver a big buffet for the bigger weekly partners lunch. Soon she was delivering lunches to other clients and catering for parties of 150 people.

Suzanne had always wanted to cook. She was born in Glasgow in 1960, the daughter of A M Ritchie, the motor trader, and grew up in Pollokshields. At Craigholme School, her top subject was cookery. She took a diploma in business studies at Cardonald College, worked briefly in the administration and secretarial department of a sawmill in Hillington, hating every minute of it, and then was taken on by Irving and Rita Rusk to open a hairdressing salon in Glasgow, but decided at the last minute not to take up the job.

Meanwhile she had met Glasgow restaurateur Ken McCulloch who encouraged her to further her culinary ambitions by doing a cookery course in London. She planned to attend a course run by a French lady in a Sussex farmhouse, but soon realised she couldn't afford to live and do the course. It was impossible to get a job in a good kitchen without experience so she planned to learn to be a chef while working as a waitress.

So in 1990, she went to London and every day for six weeks she pestered Bob Payton, the larger-than-life American who had opened the very successful Chicago Rib Shack, until he gave her a job as a waitress. She had to tell white lies about her experience (which had amounted to all of six days in Glasgow's Spaghetti Factory). Even though she was soon found out, her gumption paid off and she kept her job.

It was an auspicious place to start a career for Payton brought new ideas about front-of-house. His staff had to pass written, verbal and practical tests before they could be employed. Staff had to know about all aspects of the restaurant — who the manager was, what the concept was, what the dishes contained, where the toilets were — as well as general knowledge and they had to be salespeople as well as service staff. Payton was passionate about service and his staff needed to share that passion. They were on bonuses to sell specific dishes.

When she moved to Coconut Grove, she was earning £70-90 a week in tips, enough to finance her cookery course at the Cordon Bleu School in London. Even when she passed the course, she knew it was not enough, the rest of the school's students treated it as a finishing school, and it did not provide her with an immediate entry into a commercial kitchen. She returned to the Rib Shack and later worked in Langan's Brasserie on reception while spending her days off working for nothing in the kitchen of Blake's Hotel to develop her culinary skills.

She returned to Glasgow in 1982 at the age of 22 to open the refurbished The Buttery for Ken McCulloch and manage the front-of-house. This was a real challenge. But she felt confident about her management skills and, more importantly, she had the passion to make it work, caring deeply about the quality of food and service. She knitted together a strong team, breaking down barriers that traditionally existing between kitchen and front-of-house. Waiting staff had to know everything about the food and how it was cooked, and the kitchen staff had a share of the 'tronc' (the tips). The Buttery won accolades from the *Good Food Guide* and reclaimed its position as one of the city's top restaurants.

"I think the secret is to always treat a restaurant as if it were your own", said Suzanne. "If you can walk out at night and not think about the restaurant, then you shouldn't be there."

Two years later, she was in a position to fulfil her culinary ambitions. One Devonshire Gardens was about to open and she was offered the job of chef, cooking breakfast and meals on her own until Jim Kerr joined from The Rogano. They worked as a team for six months, with Suzanne doing prep, starters and desserts and since she lacked real experience of producing meals to order in a commercial operation leaving Jim in charge of the main courses. She kept her whites on for six months and then returned to a front-of-house role in the hotel.

In 1987, she received a phone call from Brian Turner, head chef at the Capital Hotel in Knightsbridge in London. She had worked in his kitchen for a month as a commis chef and kept in touch. Brian — later to achieve television fame on BBC's *Ready Steady Cook* — wanted her to take charge of the front-of-house in his new eponymous restaurant in Walton St.

She returned to Scotland a year later and became project manager for Dunkeld House Hotel, which Stakis was refurbishing. She was in charge of the marketing and the brochures and even spent a day stalking so that she could write about it with some authority.

In 1989 she was introduced to Ricky Daniel who owned a restaurant called The Triangle in London. It was the meeting that would, inadvertently, change her life. Ricky had teamed up with Richard McCurdie and they planned to open an upmarket restaurant in the heart of Glasgow. With 50 seats in the restaurant and 70 seats in the brasserie, it would be the most ambitious new restaurant in Glasgow in years. She was so committed to the concept that she did not take a salary for six months as it struggled to meet its financial commitments with the bank.

It turned out to be an ambitious failure and when Suzanne's father fell ill and died the next year, she felt she was at a turning point in her life. She felt her next move had to be something for herself, rather than building up and operating a business for someone else.

The obvious route was to open a restaurant of her own. It would have to be small, in the 35/40-seater range. She could not afford to set up such a venture on her own and knew that if that dream was to become a reality it would have to be in partnership with a chef. While at the time Glasgow had some good chefs, there was nobody available whom she felt had the right personality to make it work.

The impetus for her next move followed the conversation with Michael Walker of Maclay Murray & Spens. Providing some lunches did not seem such a difficult proposition, and it would take her back to her first love, cooking. Without looking further ahead, her instincts told her this could work. She knew about managing a business, she had personality and plenty of contacts. She commissioned a big, bold logo from Artwork Design.

Her instinct proved correct. She was able to develop her own cooking style, one that was appreciated by her clients. She found that her culinary skills were more than adequate for the job. She drew up her menus and distributed them alongside advertisements.

For the next few years, by focusing on quality, her business began to grow. She had to take on more staff to cope, but was still working out of her own home and she realised that she was outgrowing her existing kitchen. It reached the situation where she had the choice of taking the financial risk of moving into premises or selling up and getting out of the business altogether.

"Once I started thinking about expansion", said Suzanne, "I started thinking more about where the business was going, and about the levels of satisfaction I wanted from the business. In the front-of-house in restaurants, I had always enjoyed dealing directly with customers and I was looking for something that could effectively ally those communication skills with my culinary skills.

"When I analysed my business, I realised that, in addition to the corporate catering, I was doing a lot of cooking for my friends, who were young, but married, without the time to cook the kind of food they wanted for themselves.

"Glasgow did not have any company doing fresh food made today and being sold direct to the public and I thought there might be a gap for such a venture. It would be retailing, which in theory I knew nothing about. But I did know about restaurants and I thought of the venture as a restaurant without seats. I would have a menu and customers would choose from the menu and make up a complete meal or just particular dishes and take the food away with them to reheat at home. From the same premises I would be able to do the private and corporate catering. I also saw that actually having a shop would be good for the general business. It would give me a corporate image.

"I was out cycling one day and saw a car accessory shop in Pollokshields. It wasn't on the market, but I could see it wasn't doing well. When I went in to talk to the owner, I discovered it had already been sold. But that must have fallen through because a few weeks later it was back on the market and I took it."

The shop opened in May 1994 with a retail unit in the front, and a kitchen on a mezzanine level at the back. She took the shop on a three-year lease and the total cost of setting up the business was £28,000. She decided on a domestic kitchen, rather than stainless steel, for cost reasons, and her kitchen equipment primarily consists of cooker and oven with a central prep area. All the kitchen equipment, plus the scales and slicing machine, were leased. She hired vans when necessary, ordinary ones from her brother-in-law and refrigerated ones from Swift Auto.

She had a £15,000 bank loan and later bought the shop through a six-year interest-free loan from her brother-in-law. Since setting up the shop turnover has soared from £40,000 to £175,000 and she employs two full-time staff and three part-timers as well as 30-plus casual waiting staff. The business is split 50/50 between meals sold in the shop and private or corporate catering. Private customers have the option of collecting their meals or asking Mise En Place to do the whole dinner in their home.

A typical menu — displayed on a blackboard in the shop — would comprise five starters, five main courses and four desserts. The same menu would be sold for private dinner parties and for corporate catering, and in addition, she has a more extensive standard menu for functions. The starters might be spring onion and gruyère quiche, chicken liver pâté, fish terrine, minestrone soup, and courgette and basil soup. Main courses could be

• MISE EN PLACE •

Selections from the Menu

Spring Onion & Gruyère Quiche
Home Made Chicken Liver Pâté
Fish Terrine
Home Made Minestrone Soup
Home Made Courgette & Basil Soup

Chicken Fajitas with Salsa and Sour Cream
Salmon & Coriander Fish Cakes
Thai Chicken Curry
Chicken Lasagne
Smoked Haddock & Spinach Fish Pie

Lemon Tart
Apricot Cheese Cake
Pecan Pie
Fresh Fruit Pavlova

chicken fajitas with salsa and sour cream, salmon and coriander fish cakes, Thai chicken curry, chicken lasagne, smoked haddock and spinach fish pie, and beef tomatoes stuffed with chilli, feta, cherry tomatoes and basil. Desserts could be lemon tart, apricot cheese cake, pecan pie and fresh fruit pavlova.

The biggest outside catering job was a three-course buffet for 200 just before Christmas at Trades House for Maclay Murray & Spens. And she is seeing a growing demand from single men entertaining at home.

The bulk of the shop's retail business is in fresh food. The shop is unusual and striking in its layout. Unlike most delicatessens or food shops, it is not cluttered with every product under the sun. Rather, the non-fresh products are tastefully arranged on shelves and give the impression (as it should) that Suzanne has personally selected these products and no others for discerning clients. The Mise En Place range is distinctive and the other products include an extensive selection of Antonio Carlucci's range of Italian products including polenta, dried pasta, bagna guida and salsa. When the chef visited the shop on his book tour, it sold the most copies of his book anywhere in the UK.

It is also a shop that customers like to visit, because conversation is one of the by-products of purchasing this type of food. Customers are buying dishes for a purpose, as a complete meal, or perhaps as the beginning, middle or end of a meal in which their own cooking plays an important part. So there must be discussion, earnest or light, about ingredients and balance and texture. What else would you talk about in a food shop, but food, about what you ate last week and what you might like to try today. For cooking and eating are the simplest expressions of personality. Customers, so normally restrained in other retail outlets, provide abundant information about their lives through their simplest choices. Conversation is easy and atmosphere (the holy grail of any operation whether retail or catering) is thus achieved.

But an entrepreneur is always an entrepreneur. And on the retail side, the shop also sells a range of its own products. These include fairly obvious ideas like bread and patisserie. But they also showcase Suzanne's inbred entrepreneurial skills. For she also sells own-label herbs, but not in tiny packets or small containers with small writing, but in big glass jars whose contents are easily identifiable and which will look good in a kitchen. But perhaps the best example, because it is so simple (always the hallmark of entrepreneurial instinct) is place cards, the kind of item that nobody can ever find, and yet the obvious finishing touch for someone giving a nice dinner party.

She has already entered the food hamper market, and on a smaller scale she sells food gifts, delightfully wrapped in cellophane with ribbons which demonstrates a shrewd understanding of the value of packaging.

The business continues to expand and Suzanne is in a strong position to capitalise on her extensive experience. Not only does she have the culinary flair to develop her own cuisine, but she has a breadth of management experience to cope with the demands of success and expansion. Perhaps, most importantly, she has the front-of-house presence, the personality, that holds the entire mixture together.

THE WHISKY CONNECTION
• *Douglas Craig at Craig's Quality Catering* •

Douglas Craig's outside catering business was set up to help solve an unusual problem facing whisky distillers in north-east Scotland. Much of the marketing of whisky took place in these distilleries where special overseas guests were imbued with Scottish culture, with spectacular scenery, historic castles and, of course, the amber nectar itself. Such visits and such visitors were very important to the distilleries. They wanted to make sure everything ran smoothly and that their guests had the best of everything. And when it came to culture, castles, scenery and the whisky then there is no question that they did. But when it came to putting up their guests in local hotels and dining them, then it was just as clear that they did not.

Local hotels and restaurants seemed unable or unwilling to improve their standards to meet the requirements of visitors from all five continents who had stayed in top hotels all over the world and eaten in some of the best restaurants on the planet. The distillers wanted more control over the catering and decided it would be better to tackle the problem of accommodation and food in a different way.

The accommodation aspect would not prove too difficult. Some distillers already owned a historic building and had decided to convert these into hospitality suites for their guests. IDV opened the 35-room Drummuir Castle in the heart of Speyside and it is conveniently situated for the company's four distilleries in Knockando, Strathmill, Glen Spey and Auchroisk. Drummuir was built in 1847 for Admiral Archibald Duff who served under Lord Nelson. Chivas opened the 12-room Linn House in Keith; Macallan and Glenfarclas both created hospitality/visitor centres and Glenfiddich has recently converted a warehouse into the luxury Robbie Dhu centre which can cater for up to 200 guests.

To look after the accommodation needs of their guests, the distillers brought in their own staff. But when it came to providing top-class Scottish cuisine, they turned to Douglas Craig.

Craig's Quality Catering is the third phase in a long catering career for Douglas who was born in Ellon in 1939, the son of a classics teacher who became headmaster of Ballater a few years later. Douglas decided to go into hotel management after he saw the pleasure his mother — who was a good cook and a very good baker — had in entertaining people. He joined a traditional family business, the 36-room Loirston Hotel in Ballater at the age of 15. As all the cooking was done on a coal stove, one of his tasks was to skim coal dust from soups and sauces. The clients were wealthy visitors up for the fishing or solicitors and local businessmen. In the winter he accompanied the German chef from the family's other hotel in Braemar to the Braid Hills Hotel in Edinburgh where he was more involved in the cooking. He attended a new two-year catering course for chefs being run at the Edinburgh College of Domestic Science where Thomas Winston, the chef instructor from London, taught all aspects of preparing and cooking quality food.

He fired Douglas with enthusiasm. After Douglas achieved his City & Guilds 151 certificate and another qualification in waiting skills, he was taken on for his apprenticeship (coupled with college, this lasted five years) at the George Hotel in Edinburgh where there were 11 head chefs in a three-year period. After National Service, his first job was as a commis chef at The Dorchester Hotel in London where Eugene Kauffler was head chef. The brigade was almost entirely British and, unusually, the hotel ran a straight shifts 40-hour system with every second weekend off. Promotion was rapid and he rose from working in the roast department to larder chef, and quadrupled his pay into the bargain. The hotel ran huge banquets, easily producing 1-2,000 meals every day. He learned he was very good at organisation.

After six years he left and with his fiancée Anthea — who had been a receptionist at the Washington Hotel in London's Curzon Street — took on a management role at the Little Abbey Hotel in Great Missenden in Buckinghamshire. He was not involved in the kitchen and they only lasted six months. Deciding he needed licensed management training he joined the Chef & Brewer pub chain in 1968 after getting married. This lasted 18 months, long enough to know he did not want to work in a pub and decided to go back to his first love, cooking.

In 1970 he joined the Splinters group which had bistros in Christchurch and Parkstone in Dorset. He was offered the chance of taking a 49 per cent stake in a new venture in Lymington, Hampshire, which had 1,500 yachts in need of a good restaurant. He raised £2,000 on his own and borrowed £6,000 from the group's solicitors. The 45-seater Limpets restaurant was a cut above a bistro, with about 30 dishes on the menu ranging from fashionable food to Dover sole and steaks. But food was cooked to order, and he used very good ingredients and his larder skills were useful as he could save substantial sums by doing his own meat and fish prep and using the bones for stock. Anthea managed the front-of-house, and gained valuable experience in wine purchasing. Within a year, the restaurant was doing 200 covers a week and had entries in all the guides. He learned from good cooks and he was particularly inspired by cookery writer Elizabeth David, George Perry at the Hole-in-the-Wall and his protégés David and Sue Cumming. Local seafood and Arbroath smokies became the best-selling dishes.

But he became frustrated because he was only entitled to 49 per cent of the profits and his partners refused to let him buy them out. So he sold his share of the business to another couple for £30,000 and returned to Scotland in 1979.

But at that time prices were going through the roof and it was the end of the year before he found an affordable property. This turned out to be a Catholic Church retirement home called The Old Monastery at Drybridge. It was 600 feet up on a narrow, winding road, three miles from Buckie, but close to Elgin, Banff and Keith which all had good and reasonably prosperous populations. He knew there would be no shortage of good produce and knew that quality produce needed minimal treatment. The restaurant was planned to seat 40 with menus changing every fortnight.

"There were also 8-10 distillery groups close by and I thought they would be good for business", said Douglas. "I didn't realise how good or how important they would become later on. There was a lot of business entertaining with fishing and shooting and self-catering lodges for sportsmen. Despite its location, I didn't think I was taking a gamble. I thought I had done my homework.

"Anthea did the front-of-house, the bookwork and the wine buying. I presided over the kitchen and we saw ourselves as a couple, not as individuals. However, we kept strictly to our lines of demarcation when making decisions. We had no staffing problems due to the excellent locals.

"The restaurant did well from the start. In the summer we did the same levels as Lymington, but were not so busy in the winter. The restaurant received good write-ups, we were in all the guides again, and received special mentions for the wine list. The average spend was £12 at the beginning and £16 at the end."

The tiny bar area within the dining room did not meet the needs of the clients, so in 1984 he spent £30,000 on an extension to give the operation a bar and a lounge where light meals could be served at lunchtime and gave the guests somewhere to relax over coffee in the evening.

The end came in 1987 when he realised the potential in catering for the needs of distillers. He had been increasingly asked to do catering at distilleries. But he recognised the difficulty of trying to sustain both a restaurant and a demanding outside catering business. He did his research and realised that there would be sufficient demand for a catering operation just targeted at the distillers. He believed most distillers would be attracted by the opportunity to have someone offering a better quality of contract catering. Equally, since most distillers had good kitchens, that would minimise the need for capital investment. Just as important, marketing costs would be kept to a minimum since most of the distillers knew and liked his cooking. Word-of-mouth would be the most useful marketing tool. He sold the restaurant for £126,000 and bought a cottage in Urquhart, five minutes from Elgin, and set up Craig's Quality Catering. The cottage was developed to include a 150 sq ft production kitchen with a large storage facility. Originally he planned to do other outside functions, for which the competition was primarily local housewives. But now he tries to avoid other functions in case they jeopardise the smooth operation of the service he supplies to the distillers.

Distillers now account for 90 per cent of his business. He runs a complete contract service, providing waiting staff, as well as meals. The average spend per head is £22 and he liaises with the distiller over wines. Turnover was £120,000 in 1996 and projected to reach £130,000 in 1997. He employs 30 part-time waiting staff and two full-time and one part-time kitchen staff.

A typical visiting party, being accommodated at the distillers, will arrive on a Sunday night. Douglas will provide a hot or cold buffet with lots of fish. The distiller will provide breakfast. The party will be taken to a distillery where they will be served a light lunch by the distiller and then return when Douglas will serve up a formal dinner. The next day would be another visit to a distillery followed by a ceilidh in the evening with catering by Douglas. To

• CRAIG'S QUALITY CATERING •

Typical Evening Menu Selection

Scottish Fish Platter
Loch Fyne Oysters, Prawn Tails, Soused Herrings
& Marinated Fillets of Wild Spey Salmon

Roast Rack of Scotch Spring Lamb
with Grilled Vegetables & Sweet Pepper & Rosemary Sauce
served with Roast Potatoes and Broccoli

Drambuie Parfait with Strawberries

Selection of Scottish Cheeses & Oatcakes
Dunsyre Blue, Howgate Brie, Mull Truckle, Gruth Dhu

Coffee & Malt Whisky Truffles

prepare for the evening meals, Douglas will cook his sauces and stocks and do his basic preparation work at his production kitchen and arrive at the distillers for 6pm to do the rest of the cooking, ensuring that the produce arrives freshly-cooked to the table.

Considerable thought goes into what different kinds of visitors like to eat. Visitors from the Far East tend to eat earlier than continentals. European parties tend to stay for two nights, but Americans or Japanese can stay for a week. On average Douglas will get three or four catering jobs per visiting party. But sometimes, there will be a rush of business; at one point there were ten jobs in four days.

"The whole point of bringing visitors to the area is to give them a good time, so we have to give them what they want. There's no point us serving up what we think they want. That's the biggest change for me — from selling what is on the menu to selling what the customer wants. People from the Far East, for example, like thin soup rather than thick soup and they don't like lamb. They don't know what game is and people from America are not fond of game either", Douglas explained.

"Seafood is our most important type of food. All nationalities like seafood. Most people like fresh fish, smoked salmon and fresh salads. In general I'll create dishes from seafood, shellfish, scallops, beef, and venison.

"But the beauty of the operation is that I'm totally in control. There's no wastage because the whole meal has been ordered in advance. The biggest problem occurs when numbers change at the last minute. It's also a lot less stressful because I know when I'll be busy and I also know that when I've finished cooking for the night then my job is over. In the restaurant, I never knew when customers might arrive, especially during quiet periods. With this business, I always know. These visits have been set up months in advance and are unlikely to be cancelled. It's a lot simpler in terms of staff management. My kitchen staff are full-time but all the waiting staff are part-time, so staff aren't hanging around getting bored the way they did in a restaurant when there weren't many customers.

"There a lot of similarities to running a restaurant. In essence it's just the same except that I am dealing with a much smaller number of customers but I'm dealing with them on a regular basis and they, in turn, respect our professionalism." He added, "This business provides me with a very clear picture of what to do and where I go from here. When I started out as a restaurateur, I never thought I would become a contract caterer. But as a restaurateur I was restricted by my customers and by their eating-out experience. In my restaurants, around 80 per cent of my customers were locals and they generally wanted the same things all the time. All chefs have this problem — how do you grow as a cook when customers don't want new ideas. But with this business I have the opposite problem. My distillery guests are all well-travelled. They do not have a restricted culinary outlook, I have to keep up with them."

Keeping up with his customers has taken Douglas Craig into a very satisfying period of his catering life. But without using his entrepreneurial instincts, he would never have got there.

WORSHIP THE STAFF

• *Peter Bracewell at Drymen Pottery* •

"I never thought I'd get this far", said Peter Bracewell, gazing out at the second expansion of The Pottery in Drymen which increased the interior seating capacity from 80 to 130 covers. The Pottery is actually a tea-shop in the main street of Drymen, on the road to Balmaha on Loch Lomond and a favourite stopping point for tourists on the Trossachs run.

Tea-shops and coffee-shops have been a feature of the Scottish catering scene for decades. The bulk of tearooms never been anything more than small cafes offering snacks and beverages. For a the first half of the century, tearooms were fashionable, partly typified by the stylish Glasgow tearooms of the early 1900s when every operation appeared to have been personally designed by Charles Rennie Mackintosh and overseen by someone similar to Mrs Cranston who created the fashion. In terms of culinary fashion, the Scottish high tea was about the only type of cooking that was universal in Scotland. Rich and poor alike sat down to the same type of meal — stodgy food followed by a selection of scones, pancakes, bread and cakes. The food was presented in three-tiered cake stands with bread on the bottom, teabread above and cakes on top.

Customers effectively ate a filling meal in these kind of tearooms. But as the fashion declined and eating out became something you did at an Italian, Chinese or Indian restaurant, so the high tea business took an alarming dip. What was left was much smaller, simpler, and vulnerable to change and market forces.

A tearoom or a coffee shop has considerable disadvantages and advantages. Location is very important. There is no such thing as a profitable out-of-the-way tearoom. They depend on customer volume to survive. Therefore they need to be situated in a shopping centre or busy area in a town or city, and on a tourist route if in the country.

The curious thing about The Pottery is that is was never intended to be a tearoom. In 1967, Peter's mother converted the property from disused cottages to a pottery workshop, gift shop and first floor domestic flat. In 1985, part of the operation was converted into a 16-seater café but this was making a loss when Peter took over the business in 1987. At that time Peter Bracewell was 23 with an HND in hotel management. Food accounted for just over a quarter of the £60,000 turnover. But it seemed to Peter that food was the only way forward. His first step was to double the seating capacity and to develop the catering from cakes and beverages to simple lunch snacks and to place more emphasis on friendly service.

In 1990, he took advantage of a natural attribute of The Pottery's location and extended the building to the rear to create a 47-seat restaurant with terrace, toilets and store. Although the main door opens onto the busy main street of the village, there is another entrance at the side that leads down a wide garden path. It occurred to Peter that by placing tables and chairs in the garden he could dramatically increase seating capacity without any substantial investment, provide for overspill during busy periods, and increase the overall attractiveness of the business for the customer in good weather.

It is the aspect of the garden, rather than anything to do with pottery, which helped to develop the business. Very few tearooms in Scotland are situated in such pleasant surroundings. There are pubs with gardens, but few such tearooms outside of a stately home. And this was a real garden, with beautiful flowers and trees, rather than something that was called a garden for commercial effect.

The 1990 extension allowed him to increase the food service and add evening meals. Turnover started to grow so much so that, to cope with increasing demand, a further extension was built in 1994 to provide an enlarged 40 sq metre storeroom and four ladies toilets.

The two eating areas are quite distinct. At the front is a traditional cosy teashop with 32 seats in two sections situated next to the gift shop. There is a low ceiling and the tables are covered with oilcoths whose pattern matches the curtains. Racks of cards are within easy reach of the tables and customers usually browse in the gift shop.

The 46-seater restaurant is completely different. The glass walls and the high ceiling make the room very light and airy. However customers arrive —

• DRYMEN POTTERY •

Selections from the Menu

DAYTIME

Fruit Scone with Butter & Jam £1.40 • Chocolate Sponge £1.10
Walnut Sponge £1.10 • Flapjack £1.10 • Millionaires Shortbread £1.10
Shortbread £0.85 • Meringue with Fresh Cream £1.40
Apple Pie £1.95 • Sticky Toffee Pudding £2.35 • Ice Cream £1.30
Cappuccino £1.25 • Coffee (free refill) £1.10 • Tea £0.85
Herbal Teas £0.95 • Coke, Fanta, Sprite, Diet Coke £1.00
Milk Shakes £1.25 • Schweppes Bitter Lemon £1.00
Skol Lager (can) £1.70 • Gordon's Gin £1.30 • Wine by the Glass £1.65
Home-Made Soup with Wholemeal Roll £1.70
Home-Made Pizza £4.60-£7.50
Home-Made Shepherd's Pie Served with Chips or Baked Potato £5.10
Home-Made Lasagene Verdi Served with Chips or Baked Potato £5.10
Fish & Chips £3.10-£5.10 • Sausage or Bacon on a Roll £1.70
Baked Jacket Potatoes with Cottage Cheese £4.15
Toasties (choose any combination from Cheese, Tomato, Bacon, Onion,
Mushroom, Pineapple, Pickle) £2.20
Omelettes (choose any combination from Cheese, Tomato, Bacon, Mushroom)
Served with Chips or Baked Potato £4.45

EVENING

Home-Made Soup with Wholemeal Roll £1.60
Deep Fried Mushrooms with Spicy Dip £2.35 • Melon & Prawn £2.55
Salmon Steak with Parsley Butter £9.40
Chicken Kiev in a Pepper Sauce £7.30
Sirloin Steak served with Onion Rings £9.40
QuarterPounder served with Chips £4.15
Home-Made Pizza £4.40-£4.95 • Fish & Chips £4.85
Home-Made Lasagne Verdi Served with Chips or Baked Potato £4.85
Apple Pie with Cream or Ice Cream £2.25 • Sticky Toffee Pudding £2.25

either via a long corridor from the tea-shop or from the lane at the side — its attractions are obvious. It is very open with round wooden tables and contains an open fire. There is considerable space between the tables, more so than in the front area, for example, and this is deliberate so that what is naturally wide and open is not turned for the sake of a few extra covers into something cramped and restricted. From the restaurant can be seen the garden and white-painted metal tables and chairs for anyone wishing to sit outside.

With Scotland's weather limiting the use of the terraces, Peter decided to sacrifice the lower and least-used terrace to built a 75 sq metre conservatory connected to the restaurant. This takes indoor seating to 130 with terrace seating reduced to 30. This opened in February 1997.

The secret of a success which to some extent still baffles Peter is based on two core principles: a well-organised kitchen and good staff. The kitchen is compact and full of gadgets. Peter said he bought equipment "to solve every queuing problem and row we ever had". There are seven microwaves, three double fryers, a hot plate, a griddle, a pizza oven, four-ring burner and two toasted sandwich makers and a vacuum packer. Cakes are served from a display counter outside the kitchen as are beverages.

The menu has ten hot snacks and main courses including baked potatoes, toasted sandwiches, shepherd's pie, lasagne and soups. The cakes/desserts menu is extensive — over 20 items — and the café also sells soft drinks, milk shakes, teas and coffees. In the evening, additional dishes are available such as deep fried mushrooms, steak, salmon and chicken Kiev.

The menu has been devised bearing in mind the space, and the methodology for every dish is well worked out. For example, omelettes are made on a ring in the toasted sandwich-maker. Baked potatoes and chips are made fresh, blanched and held until required. Home-made soup is cooked in bulk and heated up by the portion in the wall of microwaves. Lasagne is made in bulk and frozen, defrosted, then microwaved at point of service. The 4oz burger is two 2oz burgers because the thinner burgers cook faster. Steaks, salmon and chicken breasts are bought and vacuum packed on site which reduces wastage.

Every area of business has been thought out. Peter buys 800lb of raspberries every year so that he can make his own jam for serving with scones. He has bought enough crockery and cutlery to last a full day because it is cheaper than hiring someone to do the washing-up throughout the day. Everything has been done to avoid crises. Everyone knows exactly what they are doing so that even under severe pressure the system operates smoothly.

"Staff are king", said Peter. "If there is a row, I will automatically apologise. It is my job to make sure nothing goes wrong. Therefore, if something does go wrong, it is clearly my fault."

This rather astonishing admission, rather than the equipment and the kitchen systems, lie at the core of the operation's success. It turns most notions of management upside down and the bulk of MBA graduates would be at least a millennium away from remotely considering such a principle.

Many businesses, the most obvious being Virgin, were founded on the idea that the most important element contributing to the success of the business was the fact that staff enjoyed coming to work because they were treated so well (and in this book, there are reflections of this ethos at the Ubiquitous Chip). But it is a more dangerous step for the management to automatically take the blame for every mistake made or caused by the staff. Most managers would rather manage without the imposition of this extra burden, which is going a shade of humility too far.

"I think a great deal of our success has come from my attitude. Don't harass your staff. I give my staff responsibility but I don't make them bear the ultimate responsibility. That transfers to me. If all managers knew they would be to blame for everything and anything that went wrong in their business — in a way that used to apply to politicians — then they would take greater efforts to ensure that nothing did go wrong", Peter explained.

"We do many things here of which I'm quite proud. We make our own jam and the cakes are all home-made. But we don't make our own coffee or our own tea. We just add the water and in quotes follow the instructions on the packet. Our coffee and tea are the same as anyone else's coffee and tea. In other words, you can get our biggest-selling products the same anywhere else.

"Making coffee — even making coffee with care — is boring. I can make that more interesting by not giving my staff unnecessary grief. What makes the difference to the business — to the bottom line — is the quality of the person serving that coffee. There are going to be times when we are so busy that everyone can't help feeling harassed. But I don't make things worse.

"What I want from my staff serving coffee or anything else — what I set as my target and theirs — is to make sure that the customer comes back. Their job is to make the customer's visit so nice that the customer wants to come back. My job is to remove the obstacles that would prevent my staff from being nice to the customer. The money the customer spends today is guaranteed, but I want to ensure tomorrow's money is as well.

"We also live in a nice world out here in Drymen. The roads are safer, the streets are safer. My staff all come from around here. That's the world they live in and they don't need me making their world intolerable by my attitude.

"It's easy for managers to act tough, in this business as much as any other. It's easier for owners to use financial pressure as an excuse for tough and aggressive management. It's easy to knock the niceness out of your staff."

There are over 20 full- and part-timers as well as himself and a manager. The part-timers are students or older schoolchildren. Younger staff are recruited at around 14-15 years of age and are trained to do the various jobs as they achieve confidence. Basic training includes how to walk through swing doors.

For the first four months, new staff do simple tasks like making milk shakes. What they do next depends on their curiosity. When they start asking how a particular dish is made, they will be shown how to make that item. As the overall system is task-oriented, it is easy for younger people to take more responsibility.

Staff can swap shifts with people doing an equally responsible job. Staff are generally friends of friends. In the restaurant, staff are not allocated specific areas. But the person who takes an order sees it through. Order slips are coloured differently for each eating area and waitpersons only come into the kitchen when summoned — either by knocking or discreet radiopaging — by a chef when the order is ready. This ensures kitchen traffic is controlled and also ensures that waitpersons are in the restaurant where they should be. Customers get free refills of coffee and this apparent generosity forces waitpersons to be on constant patrol so that they can constantly react to what is going on. It also gives the staff an excuse to talk to customers, as does an internal newsletter.

The business also has Peter's mother's pottery studio below the conservatory, which offers visitors another mini-attraction. This is a separate business from the tearoom, but it does attract the curious and is something else to visit in a village which otherwise doesn't boast a single visitor attraction. With little else to do in Drymen, the café has become a tourist attraction in its own right, attracting over 70,000 customers a year.

What it does boast is a tearoom which could, and should, attract visitors from various echelons of management to see a man who created his own catering fiefdom by making his staff king.

PICTURES ON A PLATE

• Helen Ruthven at National Galleries of Scotland •

Helen Ruthven was the surprise winner of the General Catering category in the first Scottish Chef Awards. To many in the trade, she was an unknown quantity. To those in the know, there could have been no better inaugural winner.

For Helen (along with husband Ian, who died last year) had transformed the face of catering in two of Edinburgh's most prominent art galleries — the Gallery of Modern Art at Belford Road and the National Portrait Gallery in Queen Street. The two operations average 200-300 covers a day in the restaurants and the company also carries out the catering for private views and corporate entertaining. Everything, including all the baking, is made fresh on the premises, and Helen has a commitment to quality that is clearly appreciated by her growing band of customers.

Helen was born in Glasgow and was set for a career as a civil servant until she met her future husband Ian, an art student. She shared with him a passion for food. Ian had worked in pubs and fancied owning one himself.

He had found an old boarded-up pub in Leith called Skippers that he rented as a studio, and he started imagining the potential of opening a business in this area. In the late 1970s, Leith was a far cry from its present salubrious image. Then, it was a more downbeat location.

But as Ian walked around the area, he noticed many expensive cars parked in the streets and he realised that Leith had a strong business community of professional firms and bankers who dated back to when the area was a prosperous port. It occurred to him that these professional people might well support a good pub.

Unfortunately, the pub proved a non-starter. The licensing court would not grant a public house license, but they did agree to a restaurant licence. So Ian decided he would open a bistro, a proper bistro like the ones he had seen on his European travels. Helen was very cautious about the venture. The couple bought the building for £600 and borrowed another £2,000 for the refurbishment. Ian was teaching art at the time in Wester Hailes and agreed not to jeopardise the couple's life by giving up that job. However, it proved very difficult to attract a good chef to Leith. Finally, they secured a young chef called Robin Bowie.

With conspicuous naiveté they opened the 35-seater Skippers Bistro on Christmas Eve, 1979, with a gutsy Mediterranean-style menu and an informal service style. They closed the next day, and took furniture from the bistro and various cooking utensils back to their flat for their own Christmas dinner. They opened again after Christmas. Business was very slow until just after the New Year, then the *Scotsman* restaurant critic Conrad Wilson wrote a rave review of the new bistro. Ian reneged on his promise not to give up his job and Helen, who kept hers, was roped in to take control of the accounts. Now customers were booking weeks in advance.

The business continued to grow until Ian conceived another gap in the market — this time for a wine bar. Across the road was another run-down property. They decided to sell Skippers and open the Waterfront Wine Bar. Skippers turned an enormous profit when it was sold for over £80,000 in 1982. The Waterfront was set up as a partnership between Ian and Helen Ruthven, Robin Bowie, and Sarah Reid who was the head waiter at Skippers.

The Waterfront opened with a wine bar and an outdoor eating area in summer 1982. The purchase and refurbishment cost £25,000 and proved to be another immediate success and a testament to Ian's vision. Helen did give up her civil service job a few months afterwards and later joined the company full-time.

The next year, another opportunity presented itself. The Gallery of Modern Art was opening in a new building and wanted a different kind of catering to match the new look and advertised for a franchisee to run a 70-seater café. The Ruthvens put together a successful application and moved into the contract catering business. Again, they were successful and later seating capacity doubled with the introduction of a terraced area.

Meanwhile the Ruthvens had moved to East Lothian where Ian soon believed he had found another gap in the market — this time in Haddington. He believed that a version of Skippers would work very well in this middle-

• NATIONAL GALLERIES OF SCOTLAND •

Selections from the Menu

GALLERY CAFE at the GALLERY OF MODERN ART
Minestrone £1.50 • Herby Potato Soup £1.50

Smoked Haddock Lasagne with Salad £4.45
Courgette & Hazelnut Loaf with Salad £4.10
Selection of Salads £0.95-£2.50
Baked Potato with Salad £2.50
Ham & Gruyère Croissant with Salad £3.00
Quiche or Tart with Salad £3.75

Peach & Kiwi Pavlova £2.00 • Scottish Cheeses £2.20

Selection of Home Baking & Scones £0.65 - £1.50

QUEEN STREET CAFE at the NATIONAL PORTRAIT GALLERY
Pea & Mint Soup £1.50
Fennel & Lemon Soup £1.50
Goat's Cheese & Basil Pâté with Oatcakes £2.70
Smoked Salmon & Dill Pâté £2.95

Chicken & Apricot Tagine with Salad £4.45
Caramelised Onion Tart with Salad £4.10
Focaccia with Roast Veg, Rocket & Feta £2.75
Selection of Salads £0.95 - £2.50

Strawberry Shortcake £2.00 • Scottish Cheeses £2.20

Selection of Home Baking & Scones £0.65 - £1.50

class area. He renovated a row of derelict cottages by the river. The refurbished Waterside boasted a 50-seater restaurant on the first floor and wine bar underneath.

But the bubble was about to burst. They had problems from the start after failing to exert their influence over the head chef. More worrying was the fact that they had clearly overestimated the area's potential. The town was middle-class but full of middle-class people spending all their disposable income of meeting mortgage payments. The Ruthvens nearly lost their shirts and sold in a hurry in less than a year, consolidating in the Waterfront and the Gallery.

Helen now moved into the Waterfront kitchen on a part-time basis to better understand how the business actually ran. "If you don't know what supplies are really required then you leave yourself open to abuse", she said. "When it came to fulfilling the orders for the first time, I felt nauseous but I just had to get on with it.

"Anybody can run a business, but you need to generate statistical information and be able to interpret that in order to do it properly. I learned to love figures, so that now I think nothing of spending two to three evenings a month working with figures, establishing how we are making our money, looking at the overall percentage takings, comparing this year to last. I keep a book that charts the particular events — an exhibition beginning or ending, even the onset of cold weather, anything that could affect the business one way of the other — year on year, so that I can compare figures with confidence."

The experience of cooking provided her with confidence to develop corporate entertainment business. With the Gallery, she had been worried that quality might drop if she took on any other business. But in 1990, they were asked to bid to open a café at the National Portrait Gallery in Queen Street. Their offer was accepted and the 80-seater café opened in January 1991.

Business on the gallery side has continued to grow every year, with a steady increase in the demand for corporate entertaining. Last year, they introduced a tent at the third gallery site, the National Gallery on the Mound, to capitalise on demand during the Edinburgh Festival and this proved a big success.

The secret of the success of the gallery cafés is that the food is cooked fresh in an unpretentious, interesting way, with a constantly changing menu. Everything is home-made, including scones and even jam. "We made a conscious decision", she said, "to maintain quality even if it meant looking for a lower profit."

But the success of both gallery operations had gradually been building. Overall turnover has passed half a million pounds for the first time. Turnover went up in 1996 to £554,000 from £480,000 the previous year. Revenue is in some respects related to the success of the exhibitions in the two galleries — the Annie Liebowitz Exhibition at the National Portrait Gallery was the busiest the café had ever been, but clearly the catering operations attract their own following.

But when she was invited through to an awards ceremony at the Scottish Food Proms in April 1995, Helen Ruthven did not quite believe that her endeavours would be recognised. She was wrong and received an ovation from her peers.

THE DETERMINED APPROACH

• *Andrea Barton at Barton's* •

Advice, confidence and experience are the three essential ingredients that go to make up a successful entrepreneur. Start a business without this 'ACE' package and it is inevitable that something will not work out as planned. Determination and grit will nonetheless overcome all these deficiencies, at the expense of time. Lacking all three, it has taken Andrea Barton three years to put her Barton's 24-seater operation in Kirkcaldy on the right footing.

She was born in Clydebank in 1963 but while she was young her family moved to England for 12 years before returning to Fife when she was a teenager. She was a rebellious teenager at Balwearie High School and couldn't wait to leave, attending Leven College for a year on a secretarial course, before getting her first job in 1979 as a clerk/typist for a firm of staff consultants. However, this was the start of recession and she was soon made redundant. She found her feet with her next employers, GEC Marconi. Beginning as a transport clerk, she worked her way up in seven years to become head of the company's travel department with an annual turnover of £1m.

But she wanted to get into sales, her father's profession (he ran his own successful hydraulics company), and at 22 joined Avis car rental covering an area from Nottingham to Newcastle. This proved to be the hardest year of her life as she grappled with learning sales techniques and coming to terms with being away from home for the first time in an area where she knew nobody. She worked hard building up her confidence enough to chase new business. A year later, she was promoted and moved to Edinburgh, covering sales from Dundee to Darlington.

Then she took on the job of developing a new line of business for Holland & Sherry, the Peebles-based wool merchants. Holland & Sherry were Savile

Row tailors, but the tailoring business was dying off. Anxious to safeguard their operation, the company wished to introduce into the UK an idea which had proved very successful in the United States. This was marketing made-to-measure suits direct to businessmen through their companies and in October 1988 she was hired to launch John Cooper Tailored Clothing.

She took up the challenge and remained full of enthusiasm for the fledgling business until 15 months later her father died suddenly, aged 53.

"My drive just went", said Andrea. She left her job and returned to her family in Scotland. She had toyed with the idea of opening a restaurant and decided to take an HNC course at Fife College. She enjoyed this so much — getting at last the education she had missed out on in her teens — that she followed up with an HND and then a degree at Queen Margaret College in Edinburgh and in her final year course she studied entrepreneurial skills, finance and general business skills.

But she was still undecided about a career in catering. Even with her college degree, she was finding it difficult to get a job in the industry because she was most patently suited for employment in sales. The turning point came one Friday morning in February 1994 during a visit to her hairdresser who urged her to get on with it and follow her dream. Ironically, the site she found, in Commercial St in Kirkcaldy, was a hairdressers. She took on a three-year lease at a rent of £320 a month, remortgaged her flat, negotiated a £5,000 overdraft, and borrowed from her family to raise the £10,000 required for a new kitchen, rewiring, plumbing, dry rot, toilets and decor. Her course had taught her the importance of design and she elected for a blue and soft yellow colour scheme with uplighters and logo using the initial B. Her tables were the cheapest item in the refurbishment since they were revamped school desks and the chairs came from a Masonic Hall.

Since she enjoyed cooking, her initial concept was to open as a small restaurant. Instead she opened as a coffee shop, delicatessen, sandwich take-away and, for three nights a week, a bistro. She felt that having four separate businesses under the one roof would make money. And having set it up, she lacked the 'ACE' to change. On Fridays and Saturdays, the oilcloth table coverings were replaced with white linen. She installed a long display cabinet for the delicatessen. She advertised in the local paper to announce the opening of Bartons in July 1994.

For three months business was very good. But there were problems. Since deciding on the diverse approach, she had planned to do the front-of-house

• BARTON'S •

Sample Evening Menu

Smoked Haddock Souffle £2.50
Chicken Skewers Marinated in Dijon Mustard £2.75
Dolcelatte Cheese & Garlic Mushroom Pots £2.50
Cream of Broccoli & Stilton Soup £2.25

Coriander & Garlic Chicken £7.95
Salmon Fillet with Leek & Tarragon Sauce £9.50
Fillet Steak with Mushroom & Brandy Sauce £11.00
Golden Onion & Gruyere Tartlet £6.50

Individual Pavlova £2.75
Sticky Toffee Pudding £2.75
Glazed Lemon Tart £2.50
Cheeseboard £3.00

Coffee with Petit Fours £1.50

and employ a chef. But the chef did not meet her standards and she took over the kitchen role herself from the beginning. Her initial burst of advertising started to lose its impact. The £1,000 she had invested in her delicatessen counter proved a waste of time and she dropped that side of the business. And she soon discovered the harsh truth about the location, as some of the local businesses closed. If she had been purely a restaurant, then the location would have mattered less. But a coffee shop and take-away relies heavily on passing trade. Commercial St was far from being a prominent site, although it was all she could afford.

In October 1994, the bubble burst and daytime business dropped. To make matters worse (from a professional point of view) in March 1995 she was pregnant. With a business so obviously dependent on her cooking and management skills, it was very difficult to maintain momentum with a small child. To some extent, she had to put the business on hold while she looked after her daughter Mollie (although she worked up to the day before giving birth and was back cooking in the bistro a fortnight later).

But she refused to give up and reverted to her basic business training and took a long look at the business. She was able to renegotiate the rent, which reduced overheads. Her analysis told her that the coffee shop and sandwich take-away were actually a drain on resources since that aspect of the business involved more direct labour cost and general overhead and required high volumes to be successful. The rundown of the local area suggested that such volumes would be difficult, if not impossible, to achieve, at least without more expensive promotional activity. It was becoming apparent that the business might be more profitable if it was not open six days a week as a coffee shop and draining away resources.

What seemed the most sensible option was to revert to her original plan and make more of the bistro. The bistro had been doing more consistent business than the coffee shop, even assuming that the weekends would be more busy than weekdays. With white tablecloths and candles, the place was transformed. She rated her cooking ability along the lines of a good amateur chef, but she had picked up professional techniques and her food production skills had improved as there were few complaints about slow service. The 12-dish menu changed every week and she had built up a small regular customer base. The most popular dishes include starters like crab stuffed field mushrooms and baby black pudding pancake with redcurrant and red wine sauce. Popular main courses include salmon fillet on spinach with banana and honey and korma cream, Barbary duck with orange and plum sauce, and chicken with smoked bacon and mushroom cream sauce. Best-selling puddings include dark chocolate tart, bread and butter pudding, and baked cheesecake with strawberry sauce.

She could not afford to advertise and needed to find other ways of attracting custom to the bistro. So she decided to make the overall meal cheaper for the customer by allowing them to bring their own wine in October 1996. She had a restaurant licence, but never made much on wine and thought it was a worthwhile risk. The price customers paid for the whole meal, including the wine they had bought themselves, could drop by £7-8. This was especially important for parties of customers. Or customers could decide to spend more in an off-licence buying a better bottle of wine to go with their meal. But Andrea knew there was also a trick of the mind involved that would work in her favour. Customers would not count the cost of the wine when thinking afterwards about what the meal had cost. Her cooking has also started to attract some attention and the bistro atmosphere is certainly attractive. Suddenly, Barton's Bistro was much better value for money.

Business increased immediately by 20 per cent over the previous year in the bistro and by March 1997 was up 50 per cent with customers beginning to be turned away on busy nights. The formula worked especially well for corporate and group business. Parties are particularly important to a small restaurant. Since Barton's uses school desks for tables, they are all effectively four-seater tables and cannot be split up to accommodate couples. So some nights every table could be full but, customer-wise, she would be half-empty. Now she is looking ahead with more confidence. Two full nights every week — which is all that most restaurants ever dream about — would be development enough. Now she is considering opening the bistro for lunch on selected days and/or opening on other evenings.

She has also realised, rather belatedly, that she can utilise her sales training in promoting the bistro to local businesses, especially via the telephone, which had been her primary tool while working for Avis and Holland & Sherry. She has worked out that her time might be more profitably spent chasing business during the earlier part of the week rather than running a half-empty coffee shop.

Now she is beginning to realise that her first instincts were correct and to wonder why she lacked the confidence, with her business background, to lose faith in that first tenet of enterprise — always trust your instinct. But the answer is equally transparent, many people believe that running a restaurant is somehow not a business.

Andrea Barton has now recognised that in opening a restaurant, she was dazzled by the glare of what she was doing and somehow misplaced the confidence and experience she had. But now she has them back, she can face the future as an entrepreneur.

PART THREE

Chain and Group Restaurateurs

THE CONTINENTAL APPROACH
• Pierre Levicky and the Pierre Victoire chain •

French chef Pierre Levicky went to Edinburgh in 1983 for romantic reasons. A decade later, he headed up the biggest restaurant operation ever to come out of Scotland with a turnover of £46m.

There are over 100 restaurants in a group of chains — Pierre Victoire, Chez Jules, Pierre Lapin, Marinette and Beppe Vittorio — with sites in Scotland, England, Ireland and Wales and, latterly, Belgium. Rapid expansion has been primarily due, on the business side, to a shrewd understanding of franchising and, on the consumer side, to the simple concept of good food at low prices.

It was while working at Mackintosh's and Vintner's in Edinburgh that he realised there was room for an inexpensive bistro serving quality food without expensive trimmings. The concept was born from equal parts vision and necessity.

Like most chefs branching out of their own, capital was scarce, and he gambled that consumer demand for a low-cost product would outweigh their concern about the restaurant environment. And that, in any case, there might be something intrinsically romantic about eating French cooking in what could be presented as a typical French restaurant. So he spent very little on decor, doing little more than painting the walls white, and he scoured junk shops for cheap tables and chairs, covering the worst tabletops with oilcloths. He planned to operate on charging £4.90 for a three-course lunch and £12 for a three-course dinner, prices that his catering colleagues decried as suicidal.

But Pierre was more optimistic, he had a different plan, and a different understanding of how restaurants could work. He packed in the tables, determined to maximise turnover in a business where the nature of the concept pre-determined that margins would be low. People paying his prices would be hardly likely to complain about the cramped space, especially as customers don't move around much in a restaurant anyway except to arrive and depart and make, on average, one trip elsewhere. But there was another reason for putting tables so close together. It helped create atmosphere in a city where traditionally people at the next table were regarded as at least a continent away. He felt his restaurant would not work if it was stuffy. So people were forced, by close proximity, to acknowledge customers at the next table. Proximity created conversation and strangers struck up acquaintances across the floor. In effect, since Scots were unfamiliar to a large degree with a bistro atmosphere, he was giving them something they were more comfortable with. He was actually creating a bubbling pub atmosphere. This would not be eating out in a cocoon, this would be eating out in a hubbub.

If he couldn't afford tables and chairs, he could afford marketing even less. Word-of-mouth was crucial to the success of the venture. Speedy word-of-mouth at that. The £4.90 three-course lunch was an important marketing tool. Pierre speculated that his lunch customers would do his selling for him and bring in the more lucrative dinner customers.

He was throwing down a challenge, determined to prove that interesting food need not cost a lot. But at the same time he was creating an irresistible attraction. Who would not at least be persuaded that such an idea was worth a try? What was there to lose? At those prices, it was a low-risk gamble for the customer, especially since you could eat much worse for more almost anywhere else in town. But anywhere else in town didn't have a genuine French chef at the helm. And it was odds-on that he would be given the benefit of the doubt.

Once people came, he reckoned they would come back. For the menu said it all — good food, low prices, good food, low prices, was as apparent as a mantra. Brioche filled with wild mushrooms served with smoked salmon certainly sounded good, but the price of just £3.40 made it sound even better. The same went for baked oysters with lobster, coriander and lemon zest at just £3.70, or what about baked salmon steak with ginger and spring onion for £6.50, or roast pheasant with mushrooms and port for £7.00, or even chicken supreme with lobster smoked in garlic butter for £7.20.

There was another reason for keeping prices low. Service standards in Scottish restaurants were generally poor. Customers paying £20-25 for a meal tended to demand better service, which in many cases simply meant tying up a great deal of the waiting staff's time. The main reason customers did not return to restaurants was not the food, but the service. So Pierre felt he would be much better off all round if service did not become an issue.

Pierre Levicky was born in Lyons, the gastronomic capital of France, in 1956. His mother was a teacher and his father managed a cable factory. His particular temperament became apparent during school holidays working on the production line in factory, cutting lengths of rubber tube. He was the fastest worker in the entire factory. He realised that if you did something well, you could get paid more money.

His mother worked hard during the week and Pierre and his two sisters did their own cooking. The family had a diverse culinary heritage with recipes floating around from his Prague-born great-grandmother and his Italian cousins who owned restaurants.

His first cooking job was in the local hotel where the owner was literally a huge (25-stone) personality who drove around town in first gear in a tiny Citroen 2CV and who would rush out of the kitchen with a supply of ladles if the dining room ran out of spoons. The hotel had a decidedly split personality. During the week it functioned as a hotel for commercial travellers with no cooking to speak of. At the weekend, the kitchen produced hundreds of meals and Pierre saw at first-hand how food could be both good and profitable on a large-scale. He studied catering at Grenoble. There he fell in love with a dental student from Scotland. When she found a job in northern Ireland, he followed.

Northern Ireland was the test-bed for the concept for what would become Pierre Victoire. He had been supporting himself teaching French in a school when he came across an old rundown country house hotel which had a large dining room full of atmosphere but not much else. He had a vision of a restaurant marketed as much on the atmosphere as the food. He leased the room from the owner, recruited French friends, and opened up his bistro, with good French cooking and customers sitting on ramshackle chairs. Business boomed, but the owner demanded a bigger share of the profits and Pierre decided to close the operation down.

He then followed his girlfriend to Edinburgh where he found employment in a new 40-seater restaurant called Mackintosh's, owned by Eve Thomson, a former airline stewardess, and her husband Allan (later to become a director of Pierre Victoire) who was a civil servant looking after overseas visitors for the foreign Office. The restaurant was a success from the start, won an AA rosette, and like many small restaurants turned away as many people as it could hold on busy nights. When the restaurant was sold in 1987, Pierre moved to the Vintners Rooms, but harboured his own vision of running a restaurant. Eve Thomson, well aware of his dream, took him one day in 1987 to a rundown tapas bar in Victoria Street which was on the market for £18,000. The Thomsons introduced Pierre to Alf Cattanach, Eve's bank manager at the Royal Bank of Scotland and Alf backed the project with a loan of £36,000, although the purchase price had been renegotiated downwards.

The archetypal Pierre Victoire (named after the owner and the street) was born. The ramshackle seating was matched only by ramshackle management — something that was to plague the business for years. There was no menu, prices were made up on the spot and the restaurant opened for business on its first day without a window which had broken after Pierre had attempted to dry the wet paint of the logo with a fan dryer and left it on too long.

He was 31 when the first 60-seater Pierre Victoire opened in Victoria Street in Edinburgh in May 1988, and a culinary revolution started taking shape. Lunch comprised three starters, three main courses and desserts while dinner had six starters and six main courses as well as puddings. Fish was dominant, but there was always game, chicken and beef on the menu. Fish was attractive for several reasons. Firstly, he was riding on the health boom and fish was a very healthy option and it was considered a good dish for people wanting a light lunch. Scotland also had tremendous supplies of fresh fish and shellfish and Pierre wanted to take advantage of what was best in the produce line. Fish offered the opportunity for a very diverse range of dishes. Possibly, more importantly, fish is good to cook because it can be done quickly to order. If a halibut only takes two or three minutes to cook, then you can maintain a speedier service than something which by its nature takes far longer to cook. Desserts were home-made.

Business proved to be so good that after a fortnight he was facing the toughest decision of his life. He could plough all his energies into his low-cost low-profit venture and depend on higher turnover lifting his profits. Or he could think again.

He came to the conclusion it made more sense to expand into other sites. But he had a different kind of expansion in mind to that undertaken by most chefs and restaurateurs. He had seen the problems chefs caused themselves by trying to run a second restaurant more or less on the back of the first, with the management simply ending up spreading themselves too thin and the second restaurant in danger of becoming just a pale imitation of the original rather than a true copy.

And he knew there was one very good reason why so few operations expanded beyond that pale copy. What looked like an excellent way of increasing profits has turned into not much more than a nerve-jangling and energy-sapping succession of fire-fighting emergencies. For operating even a poor imitation usually knocked the stuffing out of the owner. And any dreams the owner might have had, of running a larger empire of three or four or five restaurants, simply vanished.

Pierre had no intention of stopping at a second restaurant. He wanted more, saw the potential for expanding what was clearly a successful idea, and getting his chain off the ground before someone with more resources and manpower simply stole the idea.

So when he opened the second restaurant five months later, he viewed it as the pilot for a potential chain, and was already considering taking the franchise route for speedier growth.

Five months after the successful launch of the first restaurant, he opened another in Union Street in Edinburgh and the real learning curve began. Union Street took six months to get right. He had to create an operations system that could sustain the burden of operating a larger restaurant group in the longer-term.

The Union Street operation was deliberately run from a distance, as though it were a franchise, so that the real time-scale of identifying and solving problems could be worked out. Union Street had several problems which took time to resolve. For a start it lacked the atmosphere of the original and this forced Pierre into working out exactly what the concept was all about and to detail what conditions underlay the original idea and then to create a formula under which those could be successfully replicated in other sites. One of the problem areas identified was that the kitchen downstairs was producing food too slowly. So Pierre took the potentially dangerous step of closing the entire operation down, opening it for one day a week, then two days, then three days, until the problems were solved.

Pierre recruited all the staff and these were mostly French. This added a certain continental atmosphere to the restaurants, but also caused certain complications when that *je ne sais quoi* became too literal because few of the staff had any real command of English.

The recruitment system was simple enough. Pierre employed friends and friends of friends, often direct from France. Their lack of language skills was in some sense an advantage in that it was difficult for them to make friends right away and therefore the restaurant became the centre of their social life.

"Our staff wanted to have fun at their work", said Pierre, "and this added to the entire attraction of the restaurant. Our staff were friendly to each other and friendly to the customers. Friendliness overcame the language barrier. In the kitchen, too, we had mostly French chefs so that French was the language of the kitchen."

He had also introduced a booking system to the restaurants — standardising the number of covers per night. While this is anathema to many restaurateurs, who try to cram in as many people as possible, there were benefits in limiting customers.

For a start, it did create a sense of demand. Restaurants that are full up become places people want to go. More importantly, from an operational perspective, limiting the number of meals served meant greater control over supplies and waste and it also ensured that staff were not worn out.

With the two restaurants, he had better buying power, and was also able to take more advantage of produce bargains. He imported his own wine from France. The bulk of the wines on offer were white, dry but fruity, mostly Chardonnays and Sauvignons, and, in keeping with the pricing policy, sold in the £6-8 range. Wine mark-ups had been a constant source of customer friction in Scotland, and high prices had been a deterrent in selling wine, but Pierre's approach ensured that customers knew exactly how much a meal including wine would cost.

He had to start standardising cooking systems and chef training structures across the two units and everything was now geared towards the time when he would be operating a proper restaurant franchise.

The first franchisee was not long in coming, in June 1990. Just as the original concept had been based on low opening costs, so Pierre wanted the franchise situation to reflect that. The ideal franchisee was someone who saw the opportunity in pure commercial terms or was someone who wanted to open their own restaurant but lacked the experience to do so. Pierre felt he could supply both the concept and the experience back-up.

The location was Inverness. He had worked out that the restaurant needed a catchment area of about 60-70,000 people to survive. Pierre's view was that the first franchise should have certain in-built difficulties so that it would be a real pilot exercise. If Pierre Victoire could work in Inverness, he reasoned, it could work anywhere.

He supplied the food and chefs from among his own personnel. So head office retained quality control. He did the daily menu, working to a nightly fridge check, a basis for the food ordered from the markets the next day. Desserts were made in the Edinburgh restaurant and shipped up. He supplied the wines, taking a percentage of the sales, and he also found enough French people in the area to run the front-of-house. He also specified the kitchen and oversaw its installation.

And with so little effort expended on decor and design, the concept was easy to set up with investment capital producing returns almost from the start, rather than doing nothing for the couple of months it might take to design and fit-out a restaurant.

The keys to the Inverness unit were taken on a Monday and 48 hours later the premises were open for business. Inverness was soon catering for 45 covers a day during the week and 150 at weekends. There were differences in the eating-out culture to be overcome. Inverness people preferred meat to fish, they did not eat so much, but drank more, and wanted two-course rather than three-course meals. With Inverness well under way, he opened his own third restaurant, again in Edinburgh and by the end of his second year his turnover was £1m.

But poor management was beginning to have its effect. Lack of proper direction and poor accounting meant that he was £350,000 in debt and faced the prospect of closure. The Royal Bank of Scotland supported him through the crisis, providing a £95,000 overdraft facility on the condition that he took on a proper management team. This was the turning point for the business.

The company now has a strong team of directors — Brian Ramkin (chairman), Allan Thomson (marketing), Fiona Lawrence (franchising), Damien Brannan (finance), and Philippe Bachelet (operations) — leaving Pierre free to concentrate on developing the concepts and his vision.

Six years later, Pierre launched a pilot of a different kind. The first European venture of Pierre Levicky Ltd and the 101st restaurant of the company was a Pierre Victoire in Brussels. Instead of selling French-style cooking to the Scots, he is promoting Scottish cooking to the Europeans in one of the continent's gourmet strongholds, taking on the city's 1,500 restaurants at their own game.

Setting up this Pierre Victoire, on the trendy Avenue de la Couronne, cost £500,000 — a far cry from the cheap fit-outs of the early years.

This 350-seat restaurant comprises two main dining areas and two covered terraces. And it is Scottish in a big way with kilted bar staff and an exterior mural of a kilted piper standing beside a picture postcard scene of lochs and hills. On the walls are swords and shields and stags' heads and other Scottish bric-a-brac and one room, the Ancient Banqueting Hall, has stone floors and solid oak sideboards.

The menu is the best export promotion for Scottish cooking with haggis, cullen skink, salmon and stovies. But the cooking is far from basic. The haggis is served en croûte, guinea fowl is coated in chocolate, and the stovies are bacon and sage.

But nothing has changed on the price front. In one of the world's most expensive cities for eating out, the haggis will set customers back just £4.20 and the guinea fowl is £8.40. The set three-course lunch is £6.40 (£4.90 in the UK) and lobster is half the price of other restaurants. The average spend is just £13 (compared to £7.50 in Edinburgh). But wages are higher in Belgium — 30 per cent of turnover compared to 19-22 per cent in Scotland.

The European venture has its own director and the pilot operation is managed by a French manageress who has worked in Pierre's other restaurants for eight years. The Belgian pilot has proved a successful launching board for the European campaign. In due course, Pierre expects to set up in France, Spain, Germany and Norway. The launch itself created a mountain of publicity which helped drive in the customers. The bulk of the customers are Belgians and haggis is one of the best-selling dishes. But the operation has also targeted expatriate Scots and Burns Night and Saint Andrews Day are huge occasions and the restaurant also runs ceilidhs. Whisky is also a big seller with five good malts on offer for under £14.

Plans for stage two of the European grand plan are already under way. An advertisement for French chefs to work in the kitchens produced an unexpected publicity bounty with prime time coverage on French television and with the media embracing a new hitherto unknown (in his native land) culinary entrepreneur.

In the UK, the main thrust for expansion has come through franchising. This has largely been under the direction of Fiona Lawrence. Her brother had been a dishwasher when Pierre worked at Mackintosh's. She was multilingual and worked as a waitress in Pierre Victoire, developing such a good business

• PIERRE VICTOIRE •

Selections from the Menu (Miller Street, Glasgow)

3-COURSE SET LUNCH (£5.90)
Carrot & Coriander Soup
Crunchy Mangetout & Smoked Salmon Salad with Tarragon Dressing
Home-made Duck Liver & Pork Terrine with Onion Marmalade
Pan Fried Breast of Pigeon with Sultana & Port Wine (£1.60 supp)
Steamed Mussels in White Wine, Onion Cream & Parsley (£1.40 supp)

Baked Leg of Chicken with Red Burgundy Wine Sauce
Steamed Fillet of Cod with Tomato & Basil Concasse
Stuffed Tomato with Risotto of Vegetables, Tabasco and Sweet Peppers
Monkfish Tails served with Shallot, White Wine & Dill
Beurre Blanc (£2.60 supp)

Dessert or Fromage

Selections from the Evening Menu (Miller Street, Glasgow)

Cream of Leek & Potato Soup £1.00
Mousse of Three Fish with Horseradish & Cream Sauce £3.50
Roast Breast of Pigeon with a Port Wine & Sultana Sauce £3.80
Steamed Mussels with Lemon, Cream & Coriander Sauce £3.60

Casserole of Guinea Fowl with Mixed Vegetable, Thyme
and Red Wine Sauce £7.60
Poached Haddock with Shallots, Raspberry Vinegar and Beurre Blanc £7.20
Turbot Steak Meunière served with Pine Kernels and Fresh Herbs £8.80

Selection of Home-made Desserts £2.00
Fromage £1.70

rapport with Pierre that she was the obvious choice to entrust with the company's franchise development. The Inverness franchise had not been successful financially, but other problems resulted in Pierre invoking the break clause in the contract. The first really successful franchise was in Ayr. Expansion was helped by a £600,000 loan from the Clydesdale Bank in 1994, but now all expansion is planned to be self-financed.

The average turnover in a Pierre Victoire is now £8-10,000 a week. Average spend with wine is £15 in the evening and £7 at lunch. Restaurants generally produce a 60-63 per cent gross profit margin. Around 60 per cent of the revenue comes from food, and the restaurants remain conscious of keeping costs low, house wine is only £6.50 a bottle and champagne costs just £13.

With this kind of revenue generation, the franchise has become a considerable attraction and the company remains choosy about who they elect as franchisees. The new management team has put a proper structure into place to ensure that quality, consistency, and business targets are met. The company has a 500-strong recipe book and this is now backed up with photographs of every dish to show how it should be presented.

There are three elements to a successful franchise — the owner, the chef and the manager. Once a potential franchisee passes the initial interview, the company's aim is to make sure that chef, manager and owner can work together. They are then invited to spend a week at the Pierre Victoire training centre in Lochgelly where the company can see whether real bonding is happening.

Franchises usually run initially for five years and franchisees pay a fee of £12,500 plus 5 per cent of turnover and around £2,500 per annum to cover computer support and payroll processing. The company helps franchisees find a site and make planning applications and designing the restaurant. There is also assistance in recruiting and training. Many people attracted to the Pierre Victoire concept are people without any industry experience who see it as a straightforward way of achieving their dream.

The training centre is also utilised for training chefs and for assessing whether chefs have the qualities the company is seeking. Again these courses last a week, during which time trainees will spend periods in the restaurants as well as the centre.

The company has continued to be a strong attraction for French staff. With the recession in France, there is a surplus of chefs, so Pierre Victoire is tempting many over to Britain. Currently about half of the chefs attending training courses are French. A third of the staff in the company's Edinburgh kitchens are French.

The outlook is considerably buoyant. As well as Pierre Victoire, the company also has other concepts. Chez Jules is less sophisticated food, Pierre Lapin specialises in vegetarian food and Beppe Vittorio is an Italian concept similar in style and pricing to Pierre Victoire.

The current 106 restaurants will expand to 160-170 by the end of 1997. Apart from expanding into Europe, Pierre is also targeting the USA for 1998.

Now Pierre is looking towards flotation to fund further expansion. He had been approached to sell the company so many times that he decided to look to the City for the capital to finance expansion. An early plan to float the company did not happen, but there was a great deal of interest from prospective investors. To help develop the business, Pierre accepted a £1m investment from Abtrust in exchange for a 9.8 per cent stake. But the company could be floated on the Alternative Investment Market. Even then, Pierre is adamant that he will retain 60 per cent of the company.

KING CURRY

• Charan Gill at Harlequin Leisure Group •

On a dry spring afternoon a 20-year-old shipyard engineer was walking home along Argyle St in the Kelvinhaugh area of Glasgow. He paused to look at the menu in the window of a restaurant. While he was standing, a man appeared in the restaurant doorway and engaged him in conversation. At the end of their chat, the man, who turned out to be the restaurant owner, offered the engineer a part-time job as a barman in the restaurant at the weekends.

The engineer was hesitant. He had a good job in Yarrows, the shipbuilders, where he had worked for four years and if he had other hidden ambitions they were in the direction of a singing career. He didn't fancy wearing a barman's uniform; his colleagues at work had little respect for barmen and waiters with their bow-ties and frilly shirts. But he had always wanted to be his own boss and there was little chance of that in the shipyard. Working in a restaurant might just provide the opportunity he was looking for. The engineer took the job and that decision changed his life. It was April 1974. The restaurant was called The Ashoka West End. The engineer's name was Charan Gill.

Charan Gill's company Harlequin Leisure is now the largest Indian restaurant group in Britain with the turnover of his enterprises heading towards £10m. This benchmark will herald a phenomenal achievement in catering entrepreneurial skill, for it has been achieved with considerable hands-on input, and a shrewd understanding of how to build a business in this sector, one of the unsung areas of catering.

Charan's achievement has been to create a brand name where no one thought it possible. Indian restaurants were perceived either to be so alike as to be ubiquitous or only really marketable at the top end of the market. Charan Gill has proven that quality cooking can create its own niche providing it is backed up with a clear strategy, innovative marketing and sound business skills quintessential to the success of any operation.

Charan was born in India in 1954 and came to Scotland with his parents in 1963. His father became a bus driver like many immigrants. Charan attended school for six years and then joined Yarrows to learn a trade.

On his first Friday night as a barman at the Ashoka, he was very nervous. To his surprise, he enjoyed the job and the atmosphere. Shortly afterwards, he switched to being a waiter. He kept working at Yarrows and in his free time he sang Bhangra music with his group, the Bombay Talkie. And for five years, he lived three lives, engineer by day, waiter at weekends, singer in between.

In 1979, he left Yarrows to go on tour with the group in India. The tour was successful, too successful, for it left him with a career dilemma. Should he continue singing or was his future in catering? If he had remained in India or had been willing to move to Birmingham or London, he could have made a career out of singing.

But he wanted to live in Glasgow. He was offered a job back at Yarrow. But he dreaded living his life in the rut of a secure job. Instead, he took up the offer of a full-time job at the Ashoka West End, even though waiting was not considered a serious profession. People were waiters while they waited for some other career to happen. In the Asian community, waiting was what you did before you started your own business. But Charan believed otherwise and in due course became the manager of the 54-seater restaurant.

At that time, Glasgow was the curry capital of Scotland. Gibson Street was full of curry restaurants — Shish Majal, Koh-i-Noor, Agra, Shalimar. There were no real curry restaurants outside the city centre. The restaurants were oriented towards customer service, but few of the customers were knowledgeable about Indian cooking and the staff could more or less order for the customers.

The last two decades have seen an enormous growth in the numbers of curry restaurants. But their cultural influence in eating-out terms is much more influential. Discounting hamburger and pizza restaurants, the first serious meal most young people will have is in a curry restaurant. This usually occurs in their formative years with their parents and throughout the teenage years with their peers. After all, 'eating Indian' is now as much a part of the education process as the school curriculum.

Crowds of teenagers would not dream of going out to an European restaurant in a similar fashion. But Indian restaurants are very comforting for first time diners. If someone was trying to invent a formula for a restaurant, or looking for examples of best practice, the Indian style would be at the top of the list. Why? Quite simply, because they are almost old-fashioned in the sense that they have been created with the customer in mind, with quick, attentive service, comfortable seating and, of course, superb and affordable cuisine. They are informal and there are always plenty of staff, usually a far higher ratio than in other types of restaurants because they are often family-run. You are more likely to be asked if you want a beer or lager, rather than being asked to look at an intimidating wine list. The staff are only too eager to help you experiment with the huge variety of flavours and strengths. No dish is ever 'off', so the customer does not experience that sense of disappointment at not ordering their first-choice dish, nor that feeling or irritation that somehow the customer is at fault.

It's also a shared experience. Customers are encouraged to order different dishes, so if you don't want to risk ordering something in case you don't like it, the chances are that someone else at your table will let you have a taste. The serving etiquette supports the notion of sharing the food, as if it were some kind of family meal. In a European restaurant, each person's order is carefully laid down beside them and culinary territoriality is encouraged by definition. In an Indian restaurant, the philosophy is to share and share alike, with the dishes being placed in the centre of the table.

Curry houses have achieved a major breakthrough in terms of customer acceptance. Incredibly, people who have never eaten in a Scottish restaurant or a hotel can hold animated and informative conversations about Indian restaurants. The convenience of having an Indian restaurant in almost every neighbourhood means people can also go out for an Indian meal in the evening without having to go far, so transport costs are curtailed.

Going out for a curry is such a natural part of life these days that many people do not consider it going out at all. These restaurants also have another advantage over virtually all other establishments — including hamburger and pizza restaurants — in that the low staff turnover allows the customer to build up a relationship with the staff. This affinity keeps the customer coming back.

The real growth in Indian restaurants has been driven by a handful of restaurateurs expanding their empires. Seeking to expand the market or seeking to keep ahead of the competition has forced them to create new business opportunities, new menu ideas, new promotional ideas. The last two decades has seen a host of new food ideas ranging from eat-as-much-as-you-like buffets to balti or 'bucket-style' curries, and the restaurants have pioneered club cards, loyalty cards, discounts, and a host of other innovative ideas. Although each restaurant has its own distinct brand of cooking, the individual dishes presented are not by themselves as distinctive. The restaurants are almost throwbacks to the old Glasgow idea of eating-out which was having a good time in the presence of some enjoyable food rather than salivating over the food first and foremost; and also the idea that a meal was the start or the end of an evening out rather than something which took up the whole evening.

In the early days, restaurants were usually quiet at lunchtimes so staff only worked a 48-hour week. Many staff only came in for the evening service which made working there more advantageous in European restaurants.

Charan found the transition to full-time restaurant management fed his desire to develop a business venture. In August 1984, he was offered the opportunity to buy into the 120-seater Ashoka in Elderslie St. He raised £6,000 — including £2,000 from the bank and the rest from relatives — for a 17.5 per cent share. Weekly turnover went from £800 to £6,000 within a matter of months and went on to become the busiest restaurant in the west of Scotland. But most of the other partners were not caterers and, while financially successful, the original partnership only lasted a year. He left to take over the management of the Ashoka West End in Argyle St.

Charan did not really start to think for himself until the next year. He considered he had learned enough to be able to strike out on his own. He was confident of his management skills, but felt he lacked the cooking knowledge to make any venture a success. So he set up with a new partner, his cousin Gurmail Dhillon. Gurmail was a chef and had been with the Shanaz in Granville Street in Charing Cross for ten years. They purchased the Ashoka West End for £70,000. The restaurant took £1,600 in the first week and it snowballed from there.

For the next decade, Charan was almost always to be found at the Ashoka. He felt the place would fall apart without him. He felt it was critical for the success of any restaurant venture that there was a strong face front-of-house, someone who was always there, with whom customers could identify.

At the Ashoka he honed his promotional skills. He believed it was important to keep restaurants in the newspapers, either through effective PR or advertising, to keep the operations in the public eye. He started to develop new ideas such as clubcards. His Ruby Murray Club was a phenomenal success. Ruby Murray is slang for curry, but there was also a famous Canadian singer of the same name and Charan attracted some unexpected PR when the press assumed that his club was in fact a fan club.

He also introduced market research on customer satisfaction on the meals eaten. Managers were responsible for ensuring that half a dozen customers every day were selected for a follow-up call and asked questions about how they enjoyed their meal. In order to build up a database, the company ran free raffles. Customers calling in for home deliveries added to the database which now runs into well over 30,000, providing an ideal base for in-house promotions and marketing.

Charan was responsible for front-of-house and overall company management and Gurmail for food operations. Indian kitchens are typically divided into sections corresponding to different aspects of the menu. The role of the head chef is to organise the kitchen and the staff, to order the food, to prepare sauces and curries and to cook to order. The side chef works along with the head chef, effectively acting as a deputy. The Tandoori chef operates the clay ovens, cooking tandooris and nan breads. The fryer chef is in charge of all dishes which require frying including pakora and chapatis. There is usually also a kitchen porter.

There is a great deal of preparation in advance. But there is no central production. Such a scheme has been discussed, but it was felt that the restaurants might lose their individuality, and there would be considerable transport problems to overcome.

Chicken is the mainstay of the Indian restaurants. The Ashoka group consumes an average of 10,000lb of chicken a week. Mostly this is the front half of the bird, especially the breast which is the biggest seller. There was time when the customer was happy to accept the leg, but that's gone now, except for small drumsticks used in chicken chaat. Lamb also sells well, but seven years ago, the chain decided to take beef off the menu and therefore has not suffered from the BSE crisis. All tikka dishes are freshly cooked to order.

Considerable attention has been given to front-of-house systems. At the Ashoka, fewer waiting staff now take orders. The person in charge of a section of tables does not bring out the food, that is left to runners. Instead that waiter remains in the restaurant, ensuring that all his customers' needs are attended to. Eating habits have changed, of course. People are more inclined nowadays to share a starter rather than each having their own.

The mid-eighties was a time for expansion. In 1985 Charan bought another property in York St, off Argyle St, which he turned into an Indian restaurant called The Spice of Life. He leased a pub called the Harlequin Lounge, which traded as a normal pub without selling Indian food. The pub did good business as it was opposite a club. It was in a good location, and he bought the site for £110,000 in 1987. Both properties were sold for £440,000 so that he could concentrate on developing the Indian restaurants.

In 1988 he converted the Chequers Bar in Argyle St into Murphy's Pakora Bar to capitalise on public demand for what had now become Glasgow's two great passions — pakora and a pint, a ubiquitous snack. In 1989, he relocated The Spice of Life concept to Argyle St and turnover in this restaurant surpassed all expectations.

In the late eighties he anticipated the expansion of the curry business out of the city centre strongholds of Charing Cross and Gibson Street into the suburbs. He knew that many of the customers to his city centre operations came from far afield and it seemed sensible to assume that they would respond to an operation closer by. In June 1990, he tested his theory by purchasing the Valerio Café in Clarkston in the south side of Glasgow and opened the 40-seater Ashoka South Side. Turnover rose from £3,000 a week to £10,000 a week.

In autumn that year, he opened the Ashoka Johnstone in Renfrewshire where turnover hit £400,000 a year. In 1991, he developed the Murphy's brandname by opening Murphy's Barrelhouse in Kelvinhaugh Street as a bar-cum-diner. The following year, he took over a former Chinese restaurant in Ashton Lane in Glasgow's West End, opposite the Ubiquitous Chip, and now it currently trades at £750,000 a year. The same year he opened an Ashoka in Paisley.

Take-aways have become a growing and highly lucrative part of the business. They are very profitable, if run out of existing premises, since they require minimal staffing and space, and the product is sold at a 10 per cent discount. Many customers from as far away as Bearsden or Airdrie still regularly come into the Ashoka in Argyle Street to collect a take-away.

The proportion of take-aways to restaurant meals varies from area to area. The Ashoka South Side is 40-45 per cent take-away and Johnstone is 40 per cent take-away, but in the city centre take-away accounts for comparatively little due to the low density of inner city trading. Home delivery was a natural offshoot of the take-away business. Other companies have seen opportunities for stand-alone take-away operations and indeed Charan's brother runs the Chapati chain of take-aways.

HARLEQUIN LEISURE'S
KAMA SUTRA RESTAURANT

Selections from the Menu

Vegetable Pakora £2.65 • Chicken Breast Pakora £3.75
Poppadom £0.65 • Chicken Satay £3.95 • Chicken Chaat £3.35
Garlic Mushrooms £3.35 • Moules Mariner £4.25 • Chilli Pecuitos
£3.35
Chapati £0.80 • Nan Bread £1.70 • Raita £1.25
Basmati Mushroom Pilau Rice £2.35
Dosa with Shredded Chilli Chicken £3.75
Tarka with Aloo Channa £7.95
Chicken Tikka Breast Shakuti £7.95
Pacific King Prawns Jalfresi £10.95
Tender Lamb Bhoona Kadai £8.50
Vegetable Dansac £5.15
Prawn Dupiaza £5.85
Machi Kashmiri Style £6.45
Pacific King Prawns Ceylonese Style £9.45
Mushroom Bhaji £5.45 Paneer Shahi £5.45
Whole Tail Breaded Scampi £9.95
Penne Neapolitana £5.95
Vegetable Risotto £6.95
Sword Fish Steak £9.95
Cajun Chicken £8.95

The company also invested in a frozen food company in 1988 supplying other Indian restaurants with raw materials such as chicken and lamb rather than convenience frozen foods. The company, Maharani Frozen Foods, was relocated to Whiteinch in Glasgow in 1993 in a £1.2m refurbishment. The wholesale business had a £5m turnover. But with Harlequin Leisure Group's refocused business strategy, this does not fit within the planned growth and the frozen food part of the business has been leased out.

If the eighties were a period of expansion, the nineties were the fall-out. A price war broke out in January 1992, which in some senses was unwittingly instigated by Charan. To combat empty restaurants in the early part of the week, he adapted the kind of promotional device now beloved of airlines. It was far from being a two-for-one offer. Customers received 25 per cent off the price of a curry, but still paid full price for starters and main courses. It was a roaring success and added to, rather than detracted from, weekend business. The restaurants initially reported a tremendous upsurge in business, but then other restaurants jumped on the bandwagon and it not only lost its impact but it sparked off a fierce price war, the effects of which are still being felt today.

The price war, coupled with recession, curbed the fast expansion of curry restaurants. The fall-out was felt most by those who had invested in the sector without much restaurant experience. Many Asians from other business disciplines had invested in restaurants for the wrong reasons and did not have the experience or expertise to weather the downturn.

Charan now feels the time is right for expansion. The marketplace is growing and he is certain Indian restaurants are set to overtake Chinese. He believes it is more likely that the only kind of Indian restaurant likely to succeed now is one driven by individuals with an in-depth knowledge of the catering industry. The Ashoka is now a brand name. He purchased a site in Bellshill and the Gandhi at Charing Cross in the city centre. The city centre operation opened in November 1996 under the name Kama Sutra and has already made its name as a 'new wave' Indian restaurant.

"Now we're looking for the Harlequin Group to go further afield. The time is right to build on our strong foundation", said Charan.

"We need a new direction to take it forward. To that end Manny Hayer has come on board as operations director in charge of the day-to-day running of the group. We're planning to open 15 restaurants in three years and by the end of 1997 we expect to be the biggest chain of Indian restaurants in Europe."

The group does not have an intermediate level of managers. Each manager is in charge of a single unit. But there are two chains of command. The front-of-house managers report directly to Manny Hayer while the chefs report to Gurmail Dhillon. Gurmail has introduced group discussions with the chefs to ensure consistent standards are maintained throughout all the restaurants. The day before the group is due to meet, he will collect anonymously specific dishes from each of the restaurants and the next day the chefs will eat and comment on each of the dishes.

For the restaurant trade, there is a very low staff turnover. Full-time staff see the job as very secure. There is no chance of being laid-off. Staff tend to settle where they work. Staff who start on the south side tend to want to stay on the south side. However, the new group structure does create the opportunity for promotion as the core staff to set up new restaurants will be drawn from the existing staff. Staff work a 6-day, 48-52-hour week. The group believe it is important to keep continuity and the wages are the same for each restaurant, although tips of course may vary.

The main difference between Indian restaurants and European ones is the faster turnover of tables in Indian restaurants. Ashton Lane seats 70 people at full capacity but on a Saturday night the total number of meals served could pass 300 and some tables might turn over five times a night. This means the restaurant management team have to be very flexible.

The menu emphasis is on starters, main courses and main course accompaniments. There is little promotion of ethnic sweets. And the dessert menu is mostly ice-cream. There is a reason for this. On a busy night, serving a dessert or tea or coffee means the customer will delay his departure. The return to the restaurant from dessert or beverage is relatively small compared with the revenue from having a new customer.

With gross profit margins around 68-70 per cent, the company's pre-tax profit last year was described as extremely healthy. Part of his success is undoubtedly down to Charan's consummate marketing skills. Hardly a week goes by without some photograph in the editorial section of the newspaper. His kilt-wearing band make good copy and he made rickshaw trips around the city to generate publicity. He received national publicity for paying £5,000 for six bottles of whisky salvaged from the wrecked ship which inspired the classic Scottish novel *Whisky Galore*.

Now with the first Ashoka celebrating its Silver Jubilee, Charan is ready to accept the title of Glasgow's curry king.

SIXTY YEARS YOUNG

• *Pietro Nardini & Sons Ltd at Largs* •

There are very few restaurants in Scotland which are over 60 years old. There are buildings which are older, which have housed restaurants longer, but usually they shed owners and change names almost every decade, if not on an almost annual basis. But then, there are very few businesses of any kind in Scotland which have celebrated a golden anniversary and there are almost none which are doing exactly the same thing as when they opened. It is very difficult for a restaurant company to change its core business, and the only major change most restaurants make to their business is to shut down. When a restaurant survives so long the secret is in the branding, even in the days before branding was invented.

The Nardinis' restaurant in Largs was known by people who had never been there, although that must have been very few. Almost everyone who went to Largs made a point of going to Nardinis, it was part of the trip, a vital component part of the day out, and people arranged to go to Largs so that they could have high tea or lunch or an ice cream concoction on the West Coast's most famous restaurant. Even people who could only afford an ice-cream cone wanted to buy it at Nardinis for that entitled them to a glimpse of the famed interior and entitled them to say, of course, that they had been there.

Nardinis is not just a piece of history. To understand its success you have to look back into the history of the Scottish holiday. Between the wars, when Nardinis opened, people took their holidays, if they were lucky enough to have any, in Scottish holiday resorts, the nearer the better since that reduced the travelling costs. Most of Glasgow decamped to the local west coast resorts like Dunoon, Rothesay, Ayr and Largs. (The Edinburgh crowds went to Dunbar and North Berwick.)

This was the heyday of the pleasure steamers, carrying visitors 'doon the watter'. Families often went without their husbands, and stayed in self-catering boarding houses. The more affluent stayed in hotels. In the summer, the less fortunate made do with day trips. Evening entertainment was mundane, often only consisting, like the continentals, of a stroll along the promenade and a poke of chips or an ice cream. Day-tripper, week-ender or long-stayer, all visitors to Largs made sure their holiday was complete by sampling something from Nardinis.

Scottish holiday resorts like Largs boomed until the late sixties and the advent of cheap holiday packages abroad. If Nardinis had simply slumped or disappeared like so many holiday-town hotels and restaurants in the wake of the Spanish holiday boom, that would have been understandable, and the restaurant would have been consigned to history, perhaps an interesting historical footnote. For, of course, history had shown that every good restaurant has its heyday. Good restaurants are in the right place at the right time or they ensure that they are the popular destination.

What makes Nardinis so special is that its heyday has lasted so long, that the business has passed on from generation to generation, and that it has begun to develop other brands using the Nardini name.

Pietro Nardini, the founder of the restaurant, was born in Barga near Lucca, in Tuscany, last century. He was a door-to-door salesman of the clay statues in which Tuscany specialised. But he was more than that, he was an entrepreneur, and by knocking on some very distant doors, he soon built up a sales empire by recruiting staff in other Catholic areas like France, Luxembourg and Germany, and eventually, with his wife Rosa, came to Liverpool and Belfast.

With his savings he invested in selling soft drinks and ice cream in Glasgow. The ice cream he sold was different to that of his native Italy. In Italy, the ice cream is more water-based, more thirst-quenching because of the hot climate. But the principal ingredients of sugar, butter and cream are more suitable to the Scottish climate so Scottish ice cream is heavier and creamier than Italian.

But already he had an eye to the future. It was an uncanny eye. Long before the word trends had been invented, he saw how profitable it would be to create demand for something that did not yet exist. He could see that in the bustling Clydeside city, the men had their night out in the pub, but left the women behind. He saw the need for a venue where the women and children could go. He set up his first café to meet that unspoken demand, first of all in Glasgow, and then in Paisley. And all the while, he watched for another such opportunity, where he could be ahead of his time and profit from foresight.

Such opportunities did not come very often in one's lifetime. By then, he had brought his brothers into the business and they had opened more cafés in Paisley. But Pietro Nardini was willing to wait.

In the thirties, one of his customers owned Young's Buses, which had just started a flourishing business running day trips down the west coast. This was a novel idea at the time. Only the rich had transport and public transport did not cater to groups. But people in Glasgow and Paisley welcomed the opportunity for a scenic bus journey along the coast and back again. Mr Young felt that while his customers enjoyed the trip, there was an opportunity for something worth stopping for at the other end. By this time, Mr Young was running 300-400 trips a year involving over 10,000 passengers. Pietro had already become involved in a fish-and-chip shop and café in Nelson Street in Largs, but he saw the opportunity for something more ambitious.

Pietro Nardini's imagination went to work. He envisioned something on a grand scale, something that had never been tried in Scotland before, something that would be an attraction in its own right.

In 1934 the house and grounds of Auchenean House beside Nelson Street came onto the market. This was Lord Kelvin's summer residence, which included stables, a great lawn and living quarters, before he built his new home. And it was to be the site of the new sumptuous Nardini operation.

The three Nardini brothers sold up in Paisley and began building their grand plan. They envisioned a continental lounge café in the grand manner with a live orchestra in a building with a relaxed, sophisticated atmosphere, and a gleaming white exterior and coloured umbrellas on the terrace. The restaurant would offer fresh food, especially seafood, and in the main café customers would have ice cream, snacks and beverages.

The brothers' background in the cafés meant they were aware of the sense and profitability of opening the business all day long — even though lunch and dinner may be the busiest periods, there were always people coming in during the slack times. The key factor was that the food served in a café outside the main meal times was not labour intensive because a tea, biscuit, sandwich or ice cream could easily be prepared and served by the same person.

Cafés also attracted a great deal of take-away business before that word was invented. Cafés served ice cream and sweets on a take-away basis, and so business could be maintained at a fairly constant level. Such all-day opening was not possible in mainstream restaurants. In Largs, the brothers planned to put into operation all the good things they had learned about running a café, while at the same time making eating in the restaurant just as attractive. Even in the off-season, there was good local demand for good food in Largs itself and in nearby villages like Kilmacolm and Bridge of Weir. The plethora of products being offered to a wide range of customers at all price levels means that Nardinis operates at a very efficient level with regard to staff.

The café was open all day, but this sold more than a simple ice cream. There was a wide patisserie and bakery selection, as well as sandwiches. Even a single scoop from the extensive range of ice creams was relatively expensive, but then you were not paying so much for the ice cream as for the ambience, the interior and for just being there. And if you could persuade yourself that this was a special occasion, there was plenty to splurge on, and Nardinis had a huge range of special ice creams that was extremely tantalising. Long before supermarkets understood the principle of selling product in bulk, Nardinis was putting three different ice creams into a single product, giving it an attractive name, and selling it for a healthy profit.

The restaurant opened almost all day. Lunch was from 12.30pm to 3.00pm, high tea from 3.00pm to 7.00pm and dinner from 7.00pm onwards. The menu was enormous with over 100 different dishes, including veal, locally-caught crayfish tails and lobster, venison from Arran, game from local estates and wildfowl from the local islands. As well as individuals and small parties, there would also be coach tours arriving for a high tea or an early dinner. Such was the demand for the restaurant that a second dining-room was built just after the war.

It was an astonishing gamble and an equally astonishing success, with thousands of customers every week during season, and over 2,000 on Glasgow Fair Friday.

The boom years spanned nearly two decades from 1958 when three or four steamers a day landed at Largs, as well as bus outings and mystery tours. Customers ate Fish Teas at 2/6d or 5/- as almost a tourist package. The advent of the boom in the private car also helped. When families wanted to go out 'for a run' in the car simply because the car was there, Largs was a convenient destination and the prospect of a visit to Nardinis a good way of keeping the kids quiet in the back. The arrival of the private car had made the public more discerning. Now they could go much further afield without having to consul

• NARDINIS •

Selections from the Lounge Café Menu

Luxury Dairy Vanilla Ice Cream £1.60
Sorbet of the Day £2.00
Frappées £3.15   Flavoured Ice Cream Sodas £1.50
Baked Potato with Coleslaw £2.70
Fresh Salmon Sandwich with Lettuce & Tomato £2.30
Gammon & Cheese Toasted Sandwich £1.35
Parma Ham Salad £4.95

Selections from the High Tea Menu

Spaghetti Carbonara £4.80
Lasagne al Forno £4.95
Fried or Grilled Fillet of Haddock £5.80
Fried or Grilled Fresh Trout £7.00
Grilled Scotch Salmon Steak £8.80
Grilled Lamb Chops £6.80
Mixed Grill £8.90
Fried Veal Steak Milanese £7.50
Mushroom Omelette £5.00
Mortadella Salad £7.60
Tomato & Tuna Fish Salad £6.80
Red & Green Pepper Risotto £5.80
Scaloppa alla Marsala £9.95
Fracosta alla Pizzaiola £9.95
Petto di Tacchino alla Nardini £9.95
Tournedos Rossini £15.95
Selection of Cheeses £1.90
Meringue Glacé £3.50
Knickerbocker Glory £3.00
Scotch Trifle with Fresh Cream £1.70

timetables and be at the mercy of buses or trains. Now they would set their own agendas. Resorts became more or less attractive depending on what there was to do at the end of the trip. Compared to many other towns, Largs had an edge because of Nardinis. Even when the development of the road network made other coastal towns easier to reach, Largs was always more attractive because of Nardinis.

In its heyday, the restaurant attracted nearly a million customers a year.

But the twin development of private car and cheap holidays abroad soon took their toll and business became less dependable. And Nardinis started to look for other ways of maintaining revenue. They looked at a series of diversifications, each one developing areas in which they had developed expertise. These ranged from manufacturing refrigerated cabinets to manufacturing ice cream to further catering ventures.

During the war they manufactured parachutes. There had been an earlier diversification in the early fifties when the company opened its own bakery. The benefit of having the bakehouse is that it produces all its own bread and rolls, so that sandwiches can be made with their own bread. It makes its own wedding cakes and, in more modern times, its own pizza bases.

They opened an ice-cream factory in the early eighties with the intention of selling through wholesalers. The demand was good but in good weather they could not keep up with demand. They also ran an ice-cream kiosk in Largs as well as six ice-cream vans (loaded with 50 gallons of ice cream), but now there is only one van left. The vans used to sell 75 per cent ice cream and 25 per cent confectionery, but now they hardly sell any confectionery. Now they sell ice creams to supermarkets in Glasgow and Ayr. They bought the Golden Grill on the seafront at Largs and the Snap Basket which was an American/Italian idea with customers seated on stools.

The company also saw the potential for shop fittings, display cabinets and ice-cream machines and two members of the family were designated to set up COF Refrigeration Nardini Ltd. Initially, this venture did well, but good quality refrigerated display cabinets built to last cost £5-6,000. The trouble was many operations did not take the long-term view and instead opted for cabinets made in Taiwan at a fifth of the price that would only last two years. The operation is now scaled down.

In 1992, the opportunity came to take over The Moorings, which had been a competitor to Nardinis. Last year, Regattas opened at this venue as a café bar, a fusion of Nardini tradition with a more modern approach, and the customers could enjoy beer as much as wine and toasted sandwiches and dishes such as oysters. The café has a special menu at the weekend and special fish meals for £15-18. With room for 500 cars, and set in a leisure area with views of the hills and easily accessible for walks, it is an excellent location. Originally it was patronised by the sailing fraternity but with better marketing it has attracted a wider customer base.

The company also opened a Nardini Brasserie on the seafront, in 1995, on a site they did not own, but it proved to be the wrong location.

But they missed out on what could have been the biggest diversification of all. They were offered the opportunity to go into the pasta restaurant business in Glasgow in the sixties. But the family didn't want to go to Glasgow every day and the chance was passed up.

The family is now in its fourth generation of family management. The company is run by Fabbio (born in 1939), Pete (born in 1935) and the twins Robbie and Riccardo (born in 1951). Pete and Robbie do the administration, Fabbio is in charge of personnel and the confectionery side, while Riccardo runs the Regatta. But many other staff have spent a lifetime with the company. The restaurant head waiter Domenico Fontana has been with them for 36 years.

Management is still very hands-on. Fabbio will be up at 8am making soup and boiling crabs which must be done when they are fresh and checking stocks. Even on his day off he is partly working. He comes in first to ensure there are enough staff and to brief them on the day's business. Then he gets some sandwiches made up to go with the fruit and flask prepared by his wife. Then they drive down to Gourock for the first ferry and then he starts to relax. But the day is spent collecting mushrooms in Inveraray, Oban and around Stirling. He has a nose for mushrooms. It's a great hobby for a chef. You get to eat some, your preserve some and you get fresh air and a good walk.

The confectionery side is becoming very difficult. It's a Catch-22. In order to compete, they need to buy stock in bulk. But the stock does not move fast enough to be sold before the best-by dates. Big chocolate manufacturers no longer deliver direct to small retailers. So the company has shifted away from chocolates bars and sweets to quality fudge and tablet. The company has its own recipe for tablet and makes it on the premises. It used to make its own fudge but now this is made to its specifications by two companies, one in Perth and one in England, so that it can produce a product which appeals to its two main markets, for the West Coast Scottish taste is different to the

English in this respect. They are toying with the idea of putting a confectionery-making department in the ice-cream factory which would suit a small company. The company used to manufacture its own soft drinks, but lacked the staff to do it properly.

The original Nardinis still does 50 covers at lunch a day and 4-500 covers a day at the weekend while the Regatta does 60 covers a day at lunch. Overall, there are over 1,000 people a day eating in all the Nardini catering operations. There are about 2-3,000 coaches a year.

But the profitability has also changed. In the sixties and seventies the bulk of its high-volume items such as fish-and-chips and ice cream were also low-cost. Now the food cost is comparatively high. Originally only cold food was served in the café. But in the eighties they had to introduce hot food. The original tables were too small to use for pizzas and soups and had to be replaced.

The growth of pubs serving food has become the biggest competitive area. Nowadays the business lunch which offers a three-course meal Monday to Friday for under £5 is still very popular as is High Tea. Pasta is now very popular also.

ice cream is still a mainstay of the business. But the Nardini brand has now branched out into other areas. Nardini ice-cream counters can be found in operations as diverse as Asda and the Clifton (see page 69).

Nardinis was the original Scottish catering legend, a dynamic family business unsurpassed in its time. For many years they set the standard for Scottish catering entrepreneurs. Their vision of a glittering food temple by the sea was not just ahead of its time, but for many years set the standard for Scottish catering entrepreneurs.

NO ACCOUNTING FOR INSTINCT
• *Mike Conyers at Conyers & Co* •

For many entrepreneurs, instinct is everything. That gut feeling, that nose for the marketplace, that keen understanding of what customers want today and, more important, what they want tomorrow, such gifts are not easy to acquire. But if, like Mike Conyers, you can wrap your instincts up in the security blankets of accountancy and negotiating skills, you will have the makings of a formidable operator.

For a man who started out as a mobile disc jockey (albeit the only VAT-registered one in Glasgow), Mike has come far in 15 years in the catering business, and always at the leading edge of innovation. He opened Glasgow's first real wine bar, Lautrec's, in 1982, owned the Beacons Hotel, set up d'Arcy's Wine bar in Princes Square shopping mall, and last year had Glasgow's most successful restaurant opening with 78 St Vincent in the city centre. His next venture is as part of a consortium opening the first of a chain of American-style microbreweries.

Mike was born in 1951, the son of teachers, and grew up in Giffnock and Pollokshields, and attended Hutchesons' Grammar School. He was an early entrepreneur, helping fund his studies in accountancy at Glasgow University by operating a mobile disco. At the age of 19, he was making £10,000 a year — a substantial sum for a student in 1970. He kept up the profitable sideline long after he graduated.

He thought he was going to be an accountant for life. He worked for the Glasgow Transport Development Group for two years. But when he joined Nairn Brown Lawnmowers, he started his real business education. Nairn had gone from sharpening blades out of the back of an old ambulance in the East Kilbride area to acting as an agent for lawnmower manufacturers, finally ending up with ten agencies. Nairn was a brilliant negotiator and made Mike sit in on meetings with manufacturers.

"He would tell me what he wanted before the meeting and I watched in amazement as he got what he wanted and at the same time kept the sales agent happy too", said Mike. "He taught me never to pay the proper price for anything, always negotiate."

He moved to London to join electrical retailer Curry's as assistant financial controller, in charge of the monthly management accounts for 500 shops with a turnover of £250m, and managing a staff of seven accountants and 26 bookkeepers.

But the deeper he got into accountancy, the more he wanted out. He wanted to be his own boss. At the time, living in Teddington in Middlesex, he was eating out a lot and saw how successful the wine bar concept was proving in London. He came to believe that Glasgow was ready for wine bars and, more important, that he was ready to move out of accountancy and take his first entrepreneurial steps.

He set up a partnership with a schoolfriend, Alan Tompkins, who was selling cars for his family's car firm. The pair had previously successfully run mobile discos together.

In 1982, they found an empty ground floor and basement office in the Woodlands Terrace area of the West End and spent £130,000 converting it into Lautrec's wine bar. They invested £10,000 of their own money, borrowed £60,000 from the bank and £15,000 from the brewer, and ran up £15,000 on their credit cards. But inexperience nearly killed the project off. They missed the licensing court date, setting their opening back three months, and necessitating going back to the bank to borrow more money. Mike's accountancy background saved the day. Since he could talk to the bankers in the language they understood, they came away with another £25,000 loan.

Total capacity across both floors of Lautrec's was 260. But both areas were effectively being used as public houses, with beer and spirits expected to be the main sellers despite the promotion of the venue as a wine bar kind of operation. At that stage, the partners had no interest in operating a restaurant. A kitchen was fitted but not used, and catering was limited to cheese and biscuits to go with the wine and snacks on a small scale. For the opening in August, they had counted on 150 people turning up, but 600 appeared, so many that the guest-of-honour Lord Provost Michael Kelly could not get in. Trade was phenomenal from the start.

"Our aim was quite simple", said Mike. "Whatever else we lacked in terms of operational experience and know-how, our main aim was to make sure the customers enjoyed themselves. We wanted Lautrecs to be the kind of place Alan and I would enjoy going to and we trusted out instincts that our customers had similar tastes."

Eric Kennedy, the original chef at Charlie Parker's in central Glasgow, put them wise to the catering opportunity. So they hired him on a deal based on profit-share that quickly made Eric the best-paid chef in Glasgow. They opened up a 46-seater restaurant and soon food was 40 per cent of turnover. Sales of wine also boomed until that accounted for 25 per cent of turnover.

They repaid their overdraft within six months and with the additional profits went on the acquisition trail, buying three sites in the Broomielaw in 1984 as part of a new strategy to turn the buildings into the Nautilus Health Club. The idea was way ahead of its time — but his entrepreneurial instincts were proven correct by the health club boom of the nineties — and eventually stalled.

And in 1985, they sold Lautrec's for £310,000 to the Commercial Catering Group to fund the £375,000 purchase of the nearby Beacons Hotel. But this was to prove far from plain sailing. The first squall came when the bank only gave half the loan they had promised to upgrade and refurbish the hotel's 36 rooms.

The partners changed the name of the hotel's 88-seat La Bonne Auberge restaurant to Diva and undertook a complete refurbishment, which in hindsight did not quite work. It was a striking design with a bar of man-made white marble (Corian) and a back bar of stainless steel. But it was a city centre design that was less effective in the West End where the clientele would have preferred mahogany and warm colours. Instead the overall effect was of a dental lab with a license. The food was similar to Lautrec's and was aimed at capturing the Lautrec's market. There was also a night club/bar disco called Harveys and a function room, but they couldn't afford to refurbish the disco and had to make do with a raised floor so badly laid that it bounced when people danced. In addition, the hotel customer base clashed with that of the restaurant and the more conservative hotel customer did not like the restaurant design.

And running a hotel as opposed to just a restaurant and wine bar proved harder work than either of the partners had anticipated, especially with the constant stream of activity relating to the refurbishment. Even so, the Beacons' turnover was soon £1m, with a 10 per cent net profit. But when a good offer came in for the hotel, they were happy to let go. Selling the Beacons was also the natural end of the partnership. "The Beacons was three years wasted", said Mike. "We would have been as well putting our money in a bank and saving ourselves a lot of hard work. But I did learn to take a sharper focus on business."

Mike planned to make a fresh start in Australia but while still at the Beacons he had been approached to take over the café on the top floor of Princes Square shopping mall. In the end he lost out to Ken McCulloch for that property and instead turned his attention to a site in the mall's basement. It was an opportune decision, for instinctively he felt the basement had considerably more potential than the top floor. The basement seemed more attractive from a customer flow point-of-view.

He invested £250,000 in d'Arcy's Wine Bar. In this kind of upmarket setting, he felt he could more properly emulate the kind of wine bar he had known so well in London. The original concept was wrought iron and wine by the glass, basically a wine bar with a coffee shop/snack bar add-on. With the food element intended to be small, there was only a tiny kitchen.

The difficulty was in gauging what kind of clientele the mall would attract and what kind of catering operation would make them come to d'Arcy's. The first attempt did not appeal at all. This was a self-service operation with a horseshoe-shaped servery. Mike quickly realised that his customers did not want to queue with trays of food. So he moved into waitress service and a different kind of menu.

The operation was to include a wine-and-cheese retailer and a freshly-made sandwich shop. But the margins on retailing cheese were very small and in due course, this area was turned into a 24-cover seated area that could double as a function room. The sandwich operation, in which he invested equity, was run by ex-managers from Lautrecs who modelled their operation on the type of sandwich shop found in new York with everything made to order fresh on the premises. But this failed and was soon closed.

"But I could see that d'Arcy's was actually a far better site than I had first envisioned and that to maximise the potential, increase the spend per head, I had to look more seriously at the food side. I could see that people were interested in sitting down and eating at this location. So we devised different kinds of menus to see what the customer wanted.

"I had learned not to impose ideas on the customers, but to set up an

• 78 ST VINCENT •

Sample Lunch Menu

TWO COURSES £8.95 • THREE COURSES £10.95
Soup of the Day
Caesar Salad
Chilled Trio of Melon in a Ginger Syrup
Tomato, Rice, Olive & Mushroom Saladwith a Feta Cheese Dressing
Chicken & Asparagus Roulade served with Sour Cream

Salmon & Dill Fishcakes with a Coriander Cream
Lambs Liver with a Pepper Sauce
Cumberland Sausages served with Spring Onion Mash
Italian Meat Platter with a Red Onion Dressing
Spinach & Ricotta Tortellini with a Tomato & Basil Sauce

Strawberry Shortcake with a Raspberry Coulis
Banoffi & Meringue Cheesecake
Fruits of the Forest & Lime Ice Cream Sponge Terrine
Selection of Scottish Cheeses
Lemon Meringue Pie with an Orange Anglaise

operation where dishes could be piloted and put on the menu based on careful analysis of sales rather than leaving everything up to the creativity of the kitchen staff. We never took the good sellers off the menu, and just built things up gradually. Before computers, I used scatter sheets to help analyse what was doing well.

"I knew from the experience at the Beacons that it wasn't enough to be trendy. We give the customers what they want. And our turnover, since we opened, has never gone backwards."

So instead of a 'churn-and-turn' alcohol-led operation, d'Arcy's ended up as a mainstream food operation with a trendy bar. Excluding coffee, food now accounts for 52 per cent of turnover and alcohol only 25 per cent. The restaurant now attracts 400 covers a day and the whole operation generates £30,000 a week. The menu offers snacks and lunches during the day and a snack menu and set-price two and three-course menu in the evening.

The only mistake he made with d'Arcy's was thinking that he had created a brand. From a managerial point of view, opening a new restaurant that was already an established brand was a lot simpler than opening up one new restaurant after another. Mike reckoned that Lautrec's, the Beacons and d'Arcy's were all variations on a similar theme, and that in developing d'Arcy's he had worked much harder to cement the package, to ensure that everything worked and that he was maximising customer interest, attraction and spend. If he was going to open another restaurant, as his entrepreneurial instincts told him to do, and another restaurant preferably not in Glasgow, where he felt he might end up competing with himself, it made sense if he was able to transplant the d'Arcy's concept. He thought the d'Arcy's brand could be rolled out. So in January 1993 he spent £250,000 opening a 160-seater d'Arcy's in a 3,300 sq ft site in the Waverley Centre in Edinburgh. By June, the operation had closed down.

"I discovered the hard way that I didn't have a brand and that Edinburgh was a completely different market to Glasgow. The bar could be mobbed, packed with 300 people, but I still might only take £1,000 a night."

He paid off his suppliers and negotiated to pay off the rest of the debt over a period of time. But he still wanted to expand, but away from the bar-restaurant area into only a restaurant. He wanted about 2,500 sq ft, a 60-seater that could turn over 90 people on a busy night. He had identified that his forte was good food at value-for-money prices. And he thought there was a gap in the market for a Pierre Victoire-style operation but with everything —

quality of food, service, style, design, fittings — up a notch. He thought a value-for-money restaurant based on such principles could be a reasonable recipe for success.

He found an empty bank building on the corner of St Vincent Street and West Nile Street in Glasgow. He liked the atmosphere of the high ceilings and when a designer showed him a picture of Chartier, the famous Parisian turn-of-the-century restaurant, he knew the type of design he wanted — traditional fittings, somewhere to hang your coat, a quality look and feel. He spent £300,000 on refurbishing the building — called 78 St Vincent — which he has taken on a 25-year lease. The restaurant seated 86 on two levels. But his confidence was not high and two days before the restaurant opened, in June last year, he was so concerned that he was making another mistake that he sold off a quarter-share in the operation (which was later re-purchased).

He went for a set price menu (with supplements for more expensive dishes) so that he could offer a price guarantee to customers. The original menu was £7.95 for two-courses for lunch and £9.95 for three courses for lunch, £10.95 for a two-course dinner and £13.95 for a three-course dinner. For the first couple of months he didn't register for VAT, but when he did he simply added £1 to the menus to cover the extra cost. Supplements are added for expensive dishes like steak, brill and lobster. Interestingly, these supplements are usually £2 more expensive to have with lunch than dinner. Wines have a £6 mark-up across the board so that customers are encouraged to return on a regular basis.

His chef Andy Crawford came from d'Arcy's and devised a menu of modern Scottish dishes using fresh produce. The chef was very good at using up bits and pieces, and all the butchering is done in-house. All the staff participate in developing dishes. The restaurant runs food taste days for staff, when one of everything is cooked for the waiting staff, with the ingredients of each dish fully explained and any culinary terms. The staff taste the food, comment on taste and presentation and on the practicality of serving that particular dish in the restaurant. The system helps the chef create dishes that people want to eat, that the staff have tasted and understood, that can work within both the production and waiting system, and which the waiting staff can then promote to the customer with full enthusiasm and knowledge.

To launch the restaurant, menus were given out to businesses in a three-block radius and 10,000 vouchers offering £10 off dinner for two were also given away — of which 800 were redeemed.

The restaurant served 16 people on the first day. But word-of-mouth was very quick and now the restaurant averages over 1,000 covers a week. The restaurant has a tremendous atmosphere and the quality of the cooking has been recognised and praised. In the spring, he has expanded into the first-floor area to create 14 extra seats (bringing the total to 100) and introduce a lounge for pre- and post-prandial drinks.

In February 1997, he sold d'Arcy's. He had been thinking about selling the operation anyway, especially with the shopping mall itself being sold and the prospect of new landlords introducing changes. Someone made him an offer and he went to an agent to ask for an improved offer. Within a day, the price had risen by 10 per cent and within two days, the price had risen 20 per cent. So he sold, for an undisclosed sum, to the Carnegie Leisure Group.

By that time, he was also researching his next venture — as part of a consortium introducing the American microbrewery concept to Scotland. The microbrewery — or brewpub — has been the fastest-growing American catering concept of the nineties — and in 1996 alone over 200 brewpubs opened in the USA. If the upward trend continues at present rates in the USA, there could be more than 5,000 brewpubs in operation over the next decade.

The basis of the microbrewery is craft or designer beer brewed on the premises with the whole brewery operation an integral part of the operation's design, so that the general public believes it is in an actual brewery and can see the beer actually being brewed. The popularity of the product reflects substantial changes in the beer-drinking habits of the public, equally reflected in the trend for designer imported beers and ice beers.

The general American layout for this kind of operation usually has 3-6 different environments with a modern, relaxed feel. The first brewpub is expected to open near Anniesland on the west side of the city and close to Bearsden.

"People often ask if being an accountant is useful in this business", said Mike. "It's very good for working out break-even figures and whether an operation stands up or not and what your minimum turnover is going to have to be. And it's good for negotiating with bank managers and understanding the legal ramifications. I'm okay with management accounts and forecasting but the nuts and bolts of accounting drive me crackers.

"But what people are really asking when they ask that question is whether being an accountant makes you an entrepreneur. And, of course, it doesn't. Being an entrepreneur is much harder, and more interesting, than being an accountant."

THE GRIT BEFORE THE PEARL

Andrew Lane and John Noble
at Loch Fyne Oysters Ltd

The small boy trudged across the deserted beach, feet slipping on the wet stones, head bowed against the bitter north-westerly wind whisking along the shores of the loch. Every so often, he stooped to pick up something small from the beach and drop it into the small bag over his shoulder. He clinked as he walked, as the oyster shells he was collecting rubbed against each other. When he got home, he emptied his bag on the ground and using a heavy stone started to pound the oyster shells into grit. Then he gathered it all up with his hands and put it back in the bag. He walked into the hen yard, scattered it onto the ground and watched the hens pecking at the grit that would make their eggshells hard. That was John Noble's unromantic introduction to oysters, on his father's estate in Ardkinglas on Loch Fyne, Argyll, in wartime Britain.

Four decades later, the memory returned vividly as he discussed with a marine fish farmer called Andrew Lane an idea to grow oysters in the loch. In due course, the outcome of this discussion had international significance as Loch Fyne Oysters Ltd exported its products all round the world, but at the time John Noble had something more mundane on his mind. Recalling his boyhood chore, Noble knew that at one time oysters thrived in the loch. He was looking for an alternative to hill farming, namely harvesting the sea.

In some respects, Loch Fyne Oysters is a classic example of one of the entrepreneurial bywords of the eighties — farm diversification. Two decades ago, farm diversification was seen as the way forward for rural communities steeped in a farming tradition that was itself too traditional to be seen as entrepreneurial. Grants were readily available for all kinds of schemes that could somehow create wealth out of what had been previously grass, rock and animals.

Most of these schemes did not survive. They died for a variety of reasons. Some were too new, developing products that were burdened by having to create new markets for these products. Many were underfunded. Many were under-researched or abandoned when the burden of further research proved too great for the pocket, the brain or the stamina.

For those that did survive, what pulled them through was true grit — the determination to see something through, the ability to nurture a dream, and above all, the passion that kept them going when nothing but obstacles littered their path. Andrew Lane and John Noble could not be more different. Andrew Lane was born in Oundle on the border of the county of Rutland in England in 1951. He had always been keen on Scotland and moved to Stirling to attend university. Originally, he planned to study English literature, but at the last moment switched to biology. On leaving university, he worked on a salmon farm at Loch Striven. The salmon farm had started a hatchery on Loch Fyne where John Noble was the landlord.

John Noble was 43 years old when he met Andrew Lane. His main interest was wine and he ran two wine businesses in London as well as managing the estate at Ardkinglas. Oysters had long since vanished from the common table. Just how popular they once had been can be measured from the fact that in the 1880s the UK populace consumed 1200m — about two-thirds of the amount currently eaten in France. In the early 1800s, Edinburgh went through 100,000 a day and oyster lassies selling abundant and cheap oysters from creel baskets were a feature of the town.

Most of these oysters were from natural stocks. Industrial growth and massive consumption hastened the decline of this supply. Oyster cultivation began in Brittany in the late-19th century where beds grew the Portuguese oyster, *edulis*, originally. This was replaced in the sixties and seventies by the hardier *gigas* variety which was developed in Japan. Lane and Noble were oyster enthusiasts and simply growing oysters successfully was the limit of their ambition at that point.

"We knew it was going to be quite a long haul", said Andrew Lane, "although it turned out to be longer than we expected on the growing side."

They drew up a business plan, did a feasibility study and visited experienced oyster growers in France. The first batch of native oysters was laid down in Loch Fyne in 1978. Largely due to a dry summer and a mild winter, the oysters survived although they had been placed too far up the shore. To ensure some cash flow, Andrew worked on a trout farm in Wiltshire which also had a shop. Flushed with the success of their first experiment, they bought 10,000 seed oysters and watched with dismay as their luck ran out. Nearly all the seed died except for a few of the tougher *gigas*.

So Andrew set off for France, where the *gigas* oyster had been responsible for the recovery of oyster stocks in the seventies, to work with oyster farmers in Arcachon and further north in Brittany. But again the initial promise and excitement was tempered with the need for further experiment when many of the French methods did not translate to Scottish conditions. But still they would not give up. Gradually, after years of trial-and-error, they turned the corner on oyster farming. By that time, they were also growing other fish such as trout in seawater and the core of the business was beginning to become established. A small smokehouse was also set up so that they could supply a better range of seafood and fish to their growing clientele.

There was certainly a market for the oysters, although in the early eighties this was primarily in London mainly through wholesalers to the restaurant trade. The oysters were sent off on the night train from Arrochar packed with other seafood products to the capital. Getting them to Arrochar was the hardest part of the journey, for the steep pass of the Rest and Be Thankful was often, especially in winter, more than a match for the company's small pick-up.

Had Lane and Noble stopped there, content with developing an oyster-farming and fish-smoking business, happy to be just producers, they would probably still have been successful. But they discovered that their battle to become growers had made them more entrepreneurial. The one lesson that had been driven home by their experience in establishing the farming side was just how vulnerable they were to the weather and the marketplace.

Like all producers, they were constantly looking for ways of increasing profit from the raw produce. And they were also keen that their evangelical efforts on behalf of oysters did not simply support the misconception that oysters were a rich person's product. While Loch Fyne was far from being a destination in its own right, it was on the major road west to Oban and Campbeltown, and Lane and Noble began thinking of ways in which they could directly tap into the growing tourist traffic.

The first stab at retailing could not have been more basic—selling fish from the side of the road. Then they built a wooden hut, put empty cable drums around the hut with logs and planks forming seats and set up a fairly primitive picnic and sold passers-by tea and coffee as well as their own produce. But the picnic season was short, cut shorter than the pre-supposed Easter-to-September tourist peak by the weather.

When an unused farm building became available, they rented it with the intention of developing their business — packing, smoking and, hopefully, retailing or catering — under the one roof. The first idea was to simply transpose the picnic area inside. But it was clear that there was a public demand for a catering and retail outlet. The fact that the retailing was situated next to the smokery proved a big attraction to the travelling public. A new more ambitious idea began to crystallise in the minds of Lane and Noble.

It was clear that the general traveller liked stopping off at this little shop on the way north or south. The opportunity for the consumer to become acquainted with an apparently sophisticated product like the oyster in this unprepossessing and unthreatening environment was also a beguiling prospect. In addition, Lane and Noble also saw the potential to become a destination in their own right, a place where people would decide to stop before they set off on their journey. And it seemed quite possible that visitors could turn into mail-order customers. Best of all, a restaurant would act as a promotional device for oysters and seafood. A restaurant would also attract more media attention than just a farm, however exotic.

"The restaurant was a turning-point for us", explained Andrew. "We wanted to create a place with a sense of style. Our idea was to create the sense of being in a cabin, very close in spirit to Scotland, but also to the kind of old wooden building you might find in many a fishing village. We would use plain wood, but we wanted it to be big and airy. We knew that people had a clear image of Scotland and we saw how we could appeal to that. It was simplicity with a Scottish flavour.

"We wanted excellence in the food and a lack of formality in the interior. We wanted to be unsnobbish. We set out to create a place where people could feel comfortable arriving in walking boots or a suit. We also thought it was nonsensical to stick to standard restaurant opening hours with lunch and dinner sharply defined. We knew that we could not guarantee that tourists especially could arrange to be passing exactly at lunch or dinner time. We also thought that, for people not wanting a full meal, seafood was the ideal snack and that customers could be persuaded to eat our food at all times of the day."

The menu actually states that there is no set pattern of starters or main courses to be followed and that customers are welcome to select any dish or selection of dishes in whatever order they chose. These days, the starters choice includes three oysters for £2.60, six oysters baked with spinach and mornay sauce (£6.95), herring fillets in four marinades (£4.95), seafood chowder (£5.95). Main courses include king scallops mornay (£7.95), grilled rainbow trout (£5.95), and langoustine platter — four large langoustines, six oysters and two queen scallops — (£14.95) as well as salads, vegetarian dishes and desserts and Scottish cheeses. But at the time, they knew that they would have to convert the public.

"Oyster eating was more firmly established abroad. The French eat enormous amounts and there are oyster bars all over America with a very big one in Grand Central Station in New York, so in terms of our overseas customers, we thought we might attract the knowledgeable consumer", he added. "But we also had to survive during the winter on local business, so the informal approach definitely would help there.

"So we set out with the idea that customers could come in when they wanted and eat as much or as little as they wanted and that people who just wanted a cup of tea or coffee would be made as welcome as someone coming out for dinner. Just by using our instincts, we set out to be very consumer-friendly", explained Andrew.

"When it came to the food being cooked, again we wanted to keep everything simple. If you catch fish fresh and cook it not long afterwards in the restaurant, you are aware that it is like nothing else. With the actual raw produce so readily available, we didn't need, or want, to complicate the menu.

"We knew it could be difficult getting staff. We wanted to use local housewives in the kitchen rather than very experienced chefs who would instinctively want to do something more complicated with the food. The more complex the food became, the greater the risk that the food and the restaurant environment would not match. So we have evolved a very simple cooking style. We didn't aim to become a destination venue, and accepted from the start that our customers would always be on the way to somewhere else. Now many come just to eat here."

After their experience with the oyster farming, expectations were that the restaurant would struggle and that changes would have to be made. But the restaurant and shop was an instant success, providing the prospect of a very solid basis for the business. Suddenly, everything appeared to fall into place.

"The benefits of running the restaurant and shop were enormous because behind these we had a continuous flow of product, almost a conveyor belt running from the farm to the packer and smokery into the restaurant and shop. The waste — especially critical in a restaurant — was minimal. The cash flow benefits were also immediate. And, of course, as a company, we were able to make more money selling our produce to ourselves than to other people."

Staff-wise, the various businesses also help to balance each other out. The export side is quiet in June, July and August, just when the restaurant is reaching its peak. The export rush coincides with quieter periods in the restaurant so that staff in the restaurant can help out in the plant and vice-versa. This allows the company to create all-year, full-time jobs. This was especially crucial when the restaurant was starting out because it meant the company did not need to lose restaurant staff at the end of the season.

"What we began to develop was what became our core philosophy of buying and producing high quality seafood and selling it to all potential markets — shops, restaurants, private customers, and ourselves — at home and abroad by whatever means possible."

The restaurant quickly became a culinary delight and, more importantly, a geographic landmark. There were other beneficial by-products. It was a very good place to entertain potential buyers of the smoked or oyster products. It was also a means of picking up wholesale and export business from a tourist — one holidaymaker from Argentina now orders £80,000 of smoked salmon per year as a result of a visiting the restaurant by chance. Many visitors to the restaurant also sign up for mail-order.

The shop and restaurant also produced an expected bonus for the smokery and packing plant, helping pick up what can only be described as the 'spirit' of the operation. The next company development was a surprise. Lane and Noble decided to set up other Loch Fyne Oyster restaurants. While there was nothing new or unusual in restaurant concepts being turned into chains in the eighties, the Loch Fyne operation — so particular and so rooted in the minds of many people in that idyllic scenic tourist location on the banks of a Scottish loch — seemed an unusual candidate for such an undertaking. And yet, if you stripped away the scenery and the mythical story, you were left with a strong seafood brand. Strong branding, backed up by a strong product, was the backbone of any restaurant chain.

Lane and Noble decided the first restaurant in their expansion plan would not be in Scotland, partly so that they could be sure the concept was adaptable. The industry thought Loch Fyne would expand into places like

• LOCH FYNE OYSTER BAR (CAIRNDOW) •

Selections from the Menu

Fresh Loch Fyne Oysters £2.60 (3) • *£4.90 (6)* • *£8.90 (12)*
Six Oysters Baked with Spinach & Mornay Sauce £6.95
Eight Queen Scallops Roasted with Bacon £7.95
Loch Fyne Shellfish Bisque £7.95
Smoked Fish Pâté with Oatcakes £3.60
Smoked Salmon or Bradan Orach £5.95
Herring Fillets in Four Marinades £4.95
Fresh Salmon Marinated with Ginger and Lime £4.95
Seafood Chowder £5.95
King Scallops Mornay £7.95
Loch Fyne Kippers £4.95
Bradan Rost served hot with Whisky & Horseradish Sauce £8.50
Grilled Rainbow Trout £5.95
*Fresh Salmon Fillet, Poached or Grilled, served plain or
with a Cucumber Sauce £6.95*
Smoked Haddock Fillet Poached in Milk £6.95
*Langoustine Platter — Four Large Langoustines, Six Oysters and Two Queen
Scallops served on ice £14.95*
*Lobster Platter — One Lobster, Two Large Langoustines, Two Queen Scallops
and Six Oysters served on ice £29.50*
*Crab Platter — One Whole Crab, Two Queen Scallops, Two Large
Langoustines and Six Oysters served on ice £16.95*
*Loch Fyne Ashet — A Cold Platter of Smoked Salmon, Bradan Orach,
Bradan Rost and Gravadlax £13.95*
Grilled Pork Sausages £4.95
Home-Made Desserts £3.50
A Choice of Ice Cream and sorbets £2.90
Selection of Scottish Cheeses £3.50

Bath or Oxford. But Lane and Noble had other ideas. They wanted towns where customers were not blasé and spoiled for choice.

The first restaurant was planned in 1987 for Nottingham, where Andrew has relatives. He knew the city was very cosmopolitan with a Glasgow feel to it, with a lot of young people and not very many good restaurants. His cousin was plugged-in to the needs of the area and helped Andrew find premises. The original idea was for an out-of-town site with plenty of parking. But it was realised that a seafood restaurant would need to be busy to survive and so a smaller location was sought in town.

By Cairndow standards, the restaurant in Nottingham was tiny — a refurbished jewellers with a 40-seat capacity and no room for a shop. It was designed with Scottish pine and scenic pictures of Scotland hanging from the walls. It also aimed to attract a family market with informal service.

But remote management initially proved a problem. And they also realised that unless they had good manager, the best idea in the world would not work. The opening of Nottingham proved a nightmare due to a combination of recruitment mistakes and unexpectedly high demand for meals. But it proved that there was an unmistakable demand for the restaurant product.

The third restaurant was located in Peterborough, which has similarities with Nottingham. Again, relatives in the area provided background on the area. The town had a lot of head offices of major businesses, but few restaurants. The Peterborough operation was originally planned as a shop. The site was closer to Cairndow in style and location. It was near a busy road, not in the town centre. And with 100 seats, it was twice the size of Nottingham, but similar in size to Cairndow. The space was cheaper so they could afford to be more generous with it. And there was room for a small shop.

Of the restaurants, the original one in Cairndow remains the busiest with a turnover of about £900,000 divided equally between the shop and the restaurant. The Peterborough restaurant turnover is not far behind the restaurant turnover of Cairndow, with £480,000 of which about 12 per cent is attributable to the shop. Nottingham, which has no shop, produces around £200,000 turnover. The restaurants are all at different stages of development. Andrew feels that an extra layer of activity could be added to the Cairndow operation. The restaurant has run a successful Singapore week and French nights have also taken place. There is room for expansion in Peterborough. With the successful development of the restaurants, one way of increasing the size of the restaurant chain would be through franchising the concept.

Although this has been discussed, the restaurants at the moment do not lend themselves easily to the idea. For a concept to work, the basic idea has to be easily replicated. But none of the Loch Fyne restaurants are the same size or work in quite the same way.

The restaurants have similarities and striking differences. One area of common ground is that, despite the open-all-hours policy, most customers still have a meal rather than a snack. But average spends are different. Nottingham is £12 with Cairndow slightly higher at £12-13 (Cairndow's spend is diluted by breakfast and snacks) but the average in Peterborough is much higher, at around £17. Oysters are the biggest selling products, but in many different forms rather than just raw.

"Oysters you partly eat in your head, you eat for the idea of them", explained Andrew. "Some people are scared of raw oysters and some people are hooked. We've had to develop other ways for people to help customers enjoy oysters and overcome their fears or preconceptions.

"One way we sell fresh oysters is with a sausage. Six cold oysters with a warm sausage goes down really well. And we can offer different sausages at different restaurants — at Peterborough, for example, they prefer spicy pork. Baked oysters also sell well as they are the closest you can come, apart from raw, to eating the oyster straight out of the water.

"Oysters are also great for other reasons. They give the customer confidence in the freshness of our product. That's one way that customer preconception actually works in our favour. Everyone knows that oysters — of all seafood items — have to be very fresh. So the fact that we have them in that condition, even if the customer doesn't actually want oysters, convinces the customer in their own minds that the rest of our products will be super-fresh", he explained.

"Because we're a producer and retailer as well as a restaurant business, we can develop products for one area of business knowing that we will reap the research rewards in another. If an idea goes down well on the restaurant menu, we can think of developing it for the production side or for mail-order or for other restaurants. The next biggest sellers after oysters are our Bradan Rost hot and cold smoked salmon which is available in the restaurant and through our shops.

"Customers were initially happy just to get fresh fish and seafood, but we have to be sufficiently aware of the customer's changing needs to adapt to change. We're much more responsive to what customers want. For example, we now know that our vegetables have to be every bit as good as our seafood.

Originally, we were almost doggedly Scottish in our approach to dishes so we would have herring in oatmeal. Oysters with sausage is not in the Scottish tradition but it still fits in nicely. Marinated salmon, which we couldn't have done before, is also taking off. And we have introduced a range of wines from French regional growers. We aim to incorporate change and still not lose what makes us distinct."

The company's restaurants have also benefited from the sales drive through supermarket chains, especially with oysters. Sales of oysters in the UK have increased by £10m to £16m in the last decade, partly due to the efforts of Loch Fyne. Morisons, Waitrose, Asda and Tesco all now sell oysters where they didn't before. The rise in sales has made the prospect of eating oysters in restaurants more attractive.

The company is structured with different profit centres for each business so that no favours are done. Internal pricing is based on the best external price based on volume. The restaurant and restaurant-shop business accounts for around one-third of the company's total £4m-plus turnover. But it was the restaurant operation which drove forward a huge part of that turnover. The restaurant was the pivotal force around which the real marketing was possible.

Many businesses talk about synergy. It was one of the most abused buzzwords of the eighties. Many companies embarked on huge acquisitions in order to demonstrate a strategy of growth through synergy. Many companies spent the nineties extricating themselves from such purchases.

But Loch Fyne Oysters is a true example of synergy at profitable work. The company makes money growing and selling raw produce, it makes money smoking its own produce, it makes money selling its own produce in its own shops and restaurants and to over 400 shops and restaurants in the UK, it makes money from mail-order and export. People come to the restaurant to eat and end up buying produce from the shops. People stop at the shops for some food and end up in the restaurant. Restaurant customers sign themselves up for mail order. Mail order customers send their friends to the restaurants by the simple expedient of inviting them round to sample Loch Fyne product. Restaurant customers buy Loch Fyne product in supermarkets. Supermarkets entice customers to try oysters for the first time and the first-timers, on holiday in Scotland, put Loch Fyne on their itinerary.

The Loch Fyne Oyster experience has shown that excellence alone is not enough to put your company on the map, you need business entrepreneurial skills and above all — as every oyster knows — you need grit to make the pearl.